"AN ASTONISHING TOUR DE FORCE OF PROSE...

"... Perhaps, in the end, the book moved me because it was so clearly a triumph of faith, of faith in the act of writing. Beset by all sorts of fears ... she nonetheless went on to write the book, giving us the sensations of schizophrenia more vividly, and I suspect more honestly, than anything I've read.

She had faith in words, believing in their ability to carry inexpicable messages ... she was right."

—From the Foreword by Frank Conroy,
author of *Stop-Time*

Heart Warming Stories from SIGNET

(0451)

☐ **ALEX: The Life of a Child by Frank Deford.** The unforgettable story of a courageous little girl's battle for life against cystic fibrosis ... "Enlightening ... uplifting ... you come away richer for the reading."— *Los Angeles Times*   (131983—$2.95)*

☐ **EVERY LOVING GIFT by Judy Polikoff as told to Michele Sherman.** The inspiring true story of how a brain damaged little boy got a chance at normal life through his family's courage and dauntless determination. "First rate, vivid, gripping."—*Library Journal*   (127722—$3.50)*

☐ **THE SUITCASES by Anne Hall Whitt.** With a Foreword by Charles Kuralt. The poignant story of three little orphaned sisters shifted from foster home to foster home—until they finally found a family to love them. "Inescapably moving."—*Kirkus Reviews*   (126173—$2.75)*

☐ **A CIRCLE OF CHILDREN by Mary McCracken.** A moving story of how a teacher's dedication and love worked miracles with her emotionally disturbed children.   (134591—$3.50)*

*Prices slightly higher in Canada

AUTOBIOGRAPHY OF A SCHIZOPHRENIC GIRL

FOREWORD BY FRANK CONROY

A SIGNET BOOK

NEW AMERICAN LIBRARY

Translator's Preface

Personal retrospections of mental illness during periods of remission or recovery are not rare in either popular or psychiatric literature. Too often the rampant overdramatization, the search for appealing literary devices, the defects in recall and the confusion in sequence rob the reporting of scientific value.

In the present instance the retrospections were under control; the analyst was able not only to verify the manifest behavior but to discover the patient's specific reactions to her own progress and to the therapist's procedural errors. The recognition of such errors would alone be a significant contribution to therapeutic technique.

Mme. Sechehaye's comparison of childhood and schizophrenic thinking is clarifying, as is her review of the dynamics of regression, of ego destruction based on earliest frustrations and of ego reconstruction through the assuagement of primal needs. But transcending these in clinical importance as a practical approach to the therapy of schizophrenia is her outline of a workable system of symbolic therapy capable of returning the patient to the desired level of regression for the achievement of those satisfactions vital to further ego development.

The narrator of the story experienced a particularly early and severe form of dementia praecox, in which prognosis is usually unfavorable. Yet, without drastic physiological intervention, she seemingly recovered to normal mature adulthood. How this was accomplished will prove useful and interesting to anyone engaged in therapy.

So much has been written about schizophrenia; so little is known. From the point of view both of interpretation and effective methods, this book has much to offer.

GRACE RUBIN-RABSON
Fort Wayne, Indiana
May, 1951

Contents

TRANSLATOR'S PREFACE / 5

FOREWORD / 9

INTRODUCTION / 15

Part I: The Story

1 Appearance of the First Feelings of Unreality / 21

2 The Struggle Against Unreality Begins / 28

3 Riquette / 39

4 I Go into Psychoanalysis and Find a Mama / 43

5 I Enter the System / 47

6 The System Gives Me Orders and Things
   Begin To Come To Life / 55

7 I Am Hospitalized; the System Persists
   and I Risk Losing Mama / 62

8 I Sink into Unreality / 80

9 After a Beneficial Trip and Acute
   Crisis Confounds Me / 87

10 My First Double: The Little Monkey / 95

11 The Miracle of the Apples / 98

12 I Learn To Know My Body / 109

13 *Mama's Other Patients; All My Self-Destructive Energies Are Unleashed* / 112

14 *Mama Is Busy with Baby Ezekiel* / 122

15 *I Enter Mama's Body and Am Reborn in Ezekiel* / 124

16 *I Become Firmly Established in Wonderful Reality* / 130

Part II: The Interpretation

17 *Stages in Ego Disintegration* / 139

Development of the Pathological Perception of Reality / 141

Defense Mechanisms of the Psychotic Ego / 144

Oral Sources of the Feeling of Reality / 152

New Trauma and Massive Regression of the Ego to the Fetal Phase / 153

18 *Stages in Ego Reconstruction* / 156

Symbolic Realization of the Fetal Phase as the Beginning of Ego Reconstruction / 157

Creation of a New "Imago" / 161

Imitative Process in the Service of Ego Formation / 162

Construction of the Body Ego / 169

Affective Bases in the Structuration of the Real / 171

19 *Conclusions* / 177

Value of Symbolic Realization in Formative Mechanicms of the Ego / 177

A Dynamic Conception of the Process of Disintegration in Schizophrenia / 185

BIBLIOGRAPHY / 188

INDEX / 190

Foreword

When I began at the ridiculous age of twenty-six, to write my own memoirs, there were two books whose existence heartened me—Mary McCarthy's *Memoirs of a Catholic Girlhood*, because it proved that even a dull childhood can make fascinating reading, and *Autobiography of a Schizophrenic Girl*, because it proved that a writer could successfully re-create states of consciousness despite his failure to understand those states when they had originally occurred.

The *Autobiography* is a little-known book published by Grune and Stratton, the medical publishers; it contains a 100-page memoir by a girl named Renee and 50 pages of interpretation by her analyst. It was the memoir that particularly impressed me. In fact, despite its brevity and curiously cold style it has haunted me for years. Unlike *I Never Promised You a Rose Garden* and other relatively popular books by cured schizophrenics, Renee's memoirs are not novelistic. She made no attempt to characterize people or arrange a plot, nor did she dwell on sensual detail as a novelist might, but attempted to re-create through metaphor, and in the simplest possible language, sensations in the mind of the presumably sane reader that were in her mind while she was insane. The enormous difficulty of such a task is obvious. She writes of scenes and sensations she could not clothe in language even at the time she experienced them.

In describing one of her first attacks she says, quite flatly: "It was the first appearance of those elements which were always present in later sensations of unreality: illimitable vastness, brilliant light, and the gloss and smoothness of material things." At this particular point in the book I began to read slowly, aware that the language was highly distilled, and that despite the difficulty of her subject, Renee seemed to suggest she would make no compromises. It was up to me to struggle with "vastness" and "brilliant light" and hold them in my mind against the possibility of eventual clarification.

"One day we were jumping rope at recess. Two little girls were jumping a long rope while two others jumped in from either side to meet and cross over. When it came my turn and I saw my partner jump toward me where we were to meet and cross over, I was seized with panic; I did not recognize her. Though I saw her as she was, still, it was not she. Standing at the other end of the rope, she had seemed smaller, but the nearer we approached each other, the taller she grew, the more she swelled in size." Renee had lost the automatic use of the laws of perspective, as at other times she lost all sense of visual unity.

"I saw the individual features of her face, separated from each other: the teeth, then the nose, then the cheeks, then one eye and the other. Perhaps it was this independence of each part that . . . prevented my recognizing her even though I knew who she was." What kind of world is this she writes of—in which one can see everything and yet recognize nothing? What happens when the unconscious processes of organization and correlation associated with perception cease while perception itself goes on? Does one see less, or more?

"One day, while I was in the principal's office, suddenly the room became enormous, illuminated by a dreadful electric light that cast false shadows. Everything was exact, smooth, artificial, extremely tense; the chairs and tables seemed models placed here and there. Pupils and teachers were puppets revolving without cause, without objective. I recognized nothing, nobody. It was as though reality, attenuated, had slipped away from all these things and these people. Profound dread overwhelmed me, and as though lost, I looked around desperately for help. I heard people talking but I did not grasp the meaning of the words. The voices were metallic, without warmth or color."

These are not hallucinations. The distortions occur not in perception itself but in the act of expressing a response to those perceptions. She distorts as a man living in a four-dimensional world might distort a three-dimensional model and might say to us, "Look, I see what you see, but I see more. Here is a hint." Her metaphors are made from a floating vantage point, a slowly drifting up of intersection between different levels of reality. Thus she speaks under enormous stress, unable to tell the complete truth in the language of any single level.

Indeed, Renee was able to go back and get memories from a time when she could hardly be said to have had any functioning intellect at all, a time when she did nothing but lie for weeks in the fetal position in a darkened room—to get them, to re-create them, and to suggest through metaphor the mystery of what they meant to her. Her book reinforced my belief that almost anything was possible through language. She had gone back into another world ("another country" she called it) and surrounded the invisible with words, showing us its shape, all the while speaking in the most straightforward voice imaginable, never intruding, always relying on the reader's own mind and energy to catch the sense of what it was impossible for her to express directly.

Renee's courage inspired me also. She wrote her book very soon after her cure, imaginatively re-entering a world of which she had been terribly afraid. My own fears of reliving what had been a chaotic, frightening and confusing childhood seemed, after her example, fears I could not allow myself. She had faced her large demons; I would face my small ones. During four-and-a-half years of work on *Stop-Time*, years in which there were many violent and unexplained emotional storms battering me about, arising presumably from the solo (I was not in analysis) rediscovery of my childhood, I invoked Renee often, holding her in my mind as a nervous traveler might hold a St. Christopher medal in his hand.

But perhaps, in the end, the book moved

me because it was so clearly a triumph of faith, of faith in the act of writing. Beset by all sorts of difficulties—her fear, the impossibility of any full and direct re-creation of abnormal states of mind, the necessity of leaving out psychoanalytic language (which must have been particularly difficult), her lack of experience as a writer—she nonetheless went on to write the book, giving us the sensations of schizophrenia more vividly, and I suspect more honestly, then anything I've read. As a human document Renee's book is without doubt inspirational, but I am even more struck with it as an astonishing tour de force of prose. She had faith in words, believing in their ability to carry inexpressible messages, trusting that what cannot be said can somehow be borne aloft by what can be said. She was right.

FRANK CONROY

Introduction

This study might be considered the reverse or negative of a previous work, *Le réalisation symbolique*,* in which the case of a young girl classified medically as a schizophrenic was reviewed from the purely therapeutic point of view. The description of her schizophrenic symptoms and their disappearance demonstrated the technique effecting recovery. Formal as was the investigation, the thoughts and feelings pervading Renee's soul were readily discerned. The method of symbolic realization traced the changes brought about in her affective life; the ensuing course dependent on the therapy outlined the evolution of a psyche from its

* SEE BIBLIOGRAPHY ON PAGE 188.

regression to complete infantilism back to independent adulthood.

In *La réalisation symbolique*, however, the writer remained an observer of external manifestations, scarcely penetrating the patient's inner life. For even when the schizophrenic is in a state of physical and mental collapse suggesting dementia, he nonetheless remains in possession of his mental life and intelligence, often experiencing vivid sensations which he is unable to exteriorize.

In periods of utter lethargy or in stupor when nothing is felt, an impersonal lucidity still persists, allowing him to note not only what goes on around him but his own affective state as well. Often the extreme inertia itself prevents speech and response. The observation of what passes about him will later permit a retracing of the steps in his illness and, if necessary, a recounting of them, making possible the discovery of his life's contents, its struggles, its ineffable suffering, its pitiful pleasures, in short, a richly reactive existence belied by appearances.

Such memories must inevitably prove highly instructive for the psychologist. As Freud observed in *New Lectures in Psychoanalysis*, "These patients have turned away from outer reality; it is for this reason that they are more aware than we of inner reality and can reveal to us things which without them would remain impenetrable."

It has always been remarked that the present work may be seen as the negative of the work on symbolic realization, the exposure of what lies behind schizophrenic signs and symptoms. As the photographic negative transposes color and space values, the patient's introspections can be compared with the observer's impressions of his behavior. This juxtaposition furnishes information preventing a false estimation of the patient and the degree of his indisposition. The verbal content at times lends an impression of graver illness than does his outward appearance, and the reverse is equally true. It is always amazing to discover that the patient who seems demented is actually clear and aware of what goes on about him. There is then a tendency to blame him for his symptoms as though he could control them, forgetting that he is indeed truly powerless and irresponsible.

This renders clearer the instrinsic nature of schizophrenia, which consists in a dissociation of an affectivity deeply disturbed by the loss of contact with life from an intelligence remaining intact and acting as a motion picture camera to record whatever comes within range of the lens.

It goes without saying that Renee could

hardly recount all the impressions experienced during the course of her illness. Actually there were long periods of hebephrenic catatonia when her confusion made it impossible to register what went on either around or within her. During periods of aggravated stupor no memory traces of perceptive impressions remained. For this reason, in narrating Renee's intimate introspections, introspections which seem to bear witness to an astonishing lucidity, it is not to be forgotten that they represent only certain periods of her illness, fortunately, those most interesting from the psychological angle.

MARGUERITE SECHEHAYE

PART I

THE STORY

Appearance of the First
Feelings of Unreality

[This is Renee's intimate story as she recounted it shortly after her recovery. It begins with her first feelings of unreality when she was five years old.]

1 I remember very well the day it happened. We were staying in the country and I had gone for a walk alone as I did now and then. Suddenly, as I was passing the school, I heard a German song; the children were having a singing lesson. I stopped to listen, and at that instant a strange feeling came over me, a feeling hard to analyze but akin to something I was to know too well later—a disturbing sense of unreality. It seemed to me that I no longer recognized the school, it had become as large as a barracks; the singing children were prisoners, compelled to sing. It was as though the school and the children's song were set apart from the rest of the world. At the same time my eye encountered a field of wheat whose limits I could not see. The song of the children imprisoned in the smooth stone school-barracks filled me with such anxiety that I broke into sobs. I ran home to our garden and began to play "to make things seem as they usually were," that is, to return to reality. It was the first appearance of those elements which were always present in later sensations and unreality: illimitable vast-ness, brilliant light, and the gloss and smoothness of material things. I have no explanation for what happened, or why. But it was during this same period that I learned my father had a mistress and that he made my mother cry. This revelation bowled me over because I had heard my mother say that if my father left her, she would kill herself.

[In the years that followed until she was about twelve, Renee experienced unreal feelings many times. From then on, the sensations became more and more intense, more and more frequent. She remembers that the most striking of these was related to school, the school she had attended for two years.]

One day we were jumping rope at recess. Two little girls were turning a long rope while two others jumped in from either side to meet and cross over. When it came my turn and I saw my partner jump toward me where we were to meet and cross over, I was seized with panic; I did not recognize her. Though I saw her as she was, still, it was not she. Standing at the other end of the rope, she had seemed smaller, but the nearer we approached each other, the taller she grew, the more she swelled in size.

I cried out, "Stop, Alice, you look like a lion; you frighten me!" At the sound of the fear in my voice which I tried to dissemble under the guise of fooling, the game came to an abrupt halt. The girls looked at me, amazed, and said, "You're silly—Alice, a lion? You don't know what you're talking about."

Then the game began again. Once more my playmate became strangely transformed and, with an excited laugh, once more I cried out, "Stop, Alice, I'm afraid of you; you're a lion!" But actually, I didn't see a lion at all: it was only an attempt to describe the enlarging image of my friend and the fact that I didn't recognize her. Suddenly I saw the resemblance of this phenomenon to my nightmare of "the needle in the hay."

It was a dream that recurred often, especially when I was feverish, and it caused me the most frightful anguish. Later I always associated my unreal perceptions with the dream of the needle.

Here is the dream: A barn, brilliantly illuminated by electricity. The walls painted white, smooth—smooth and shining. In the immensity, a needle—fine, pointed, hard, glittering in the light. The needle in the emptiness filled me with excruciating terror. Then a haystack fills up the emptiness and engulfs the needle. The haystack, small at first, swells and swells and in the center, the needle, endowed with tremendous electrical force, communicates its charge to the hay. The electrical current,* the invasion by the hay, and the blinding light* combine to augment the fear to a paroxysm of terror and I wake up screaming, "The needle, the needle!"

What happened during the rope game was the same sort of thing: tension, something growing inordinately, and anxiety.

---

*The dual nature of *éclairé* meaning both lighted in the physical and enlightened in the intellectual sense, and of *tension* used here both as state of tension and as electrical current, perhaps plays a part in Renee's fantasy not immediately apparent in translation from the French.

From then on, the recreation period at school was often a source of the unreal feeling. I kept close to the fence as though I were indeed a prisoner and watched the other pupils shouting and running about in the school yard. They looked to me like ants under a bright light. The school building became immense, smooth, unreal, and an inexpressible anguish pressed in on me. I fancied that the people watching us from the street thought all of us were prisoners just as I was a prisoner and I wanted so much to escape. Sometimes I shook the grating as though there were no other way out, like a madman, I thought, who wanted to return to real life.

For the street seemed alive, gay and real, and the people moving there were living and real people, while all that was within the confines of the yard was limitless, unreal, mechanical and without meaning: it was the nightmare of the needle in the hay.

I caught myself in this state only in the yard, never in class. I suffered from it horribly but I did not know how to get free. Play, conversation, reading—nothing seemed able to break the unreal circle that surrounded me.

These crises, far from abating, seemed rather to increase. One day, while I was in the principal's office, suddenly the room became enormous, illuminated by a dreadful electric light that cast false shadows. Everything was exact, smooth, artificial, extremely tense; the chairs and tables seemed models placed here and there. Pupils and teachers were puppets revolving without cause, without objective. I recognized nothing, nobody. It was as though reality, attenuated, had slipped away from all these things and these people. Profound dread overwhelmed me, and as though lost, I looked around desperately for help. I heard people talking but I did not grasp the meaning of the words. The voices were metallic, without warmth or color. From time to time, a word detached itself from the rest. It repeated itself over and over in my head, absurd, as though cut off by a knife. And when one of my schoolmates came toward me, I saw her grow larger and larger, like the haystack.

I went to my teacher and said to her, "I am afraid because everyone has a tiny crow's head on his head." She smiled gently at me and answered something I don't remember. But her smile, instead of reassuring me, only increased the anxiety and confusion for I saw her teeth, white and even in the gleam of the light. Remaining all the while like themselves, soon they monopolized my entire vision as if the whole room were nothing but teeth under a remorseless light. Ghastly fear gripped me.

What saved me that day was activity. It was the hour to go to chapel for prayer, and like the other children I had to get in line. To move, to change the scene, to do something definite and customary, helped a great deal. Nevertheless, I took the unreal state to chapel with me, though to a lesser degree. That evening I was completely exhausted.

The remarkable thing was that, when I chanced to return to reality, I thought no more of these terrible moments. I did not forget them, but I did not think of them. And still, they were repeated very frequently, pervading a larger and larger segment of my life.

The Struggle Against
Unreality Begins

2   From the point of view of scholarship, my last year at the elementary school was good enough. I took three prizes, two of them firsts. I seemed to have, then, everything necessary for success in the secondary school. Unfortunately, this was not the case, and the cause lay in the "unreality."

At first I had trouble in adjusting to the schedule and to the new teaching procedure. Then three subjects literally terrified me: singing, drawing, and calisthenics, and I might even add sewing.

It seems that I had a pleasant high soprano voice and the teacher counted on me for solo parts in the chorus. But he noticed pretty soon that I sang off key, singing sharp or flat as much as a whole step or two when I wasn't watching. Furthermore, I was unable either to learn solfeggio, to beat the measure or to keep the rhythm.

These lessons aroused an immeasurable anxiety quite disproportionate to the cause. It was the same in drawing. I don't know what happened during the summer vacation, but I seemed to have lost a sense of perspective. So I copied the model from a schoolmate's sketch, thus lending a false perspective from where I sat.

In the gymnasium I didn't understand the commands, confusing left and right. As for the sewing lesson, it was impossible to understand the technique of placing patches or the mysteries of knitting a sock heel. Varied as these subjects were, they presented similar problems, so that more and more, despite my efforts, I lost the feeling of practical things.

In these disturbing circumstances I sensed again the atmosphere of unreality. During class, in the quiet of the work period, I heard the street noises—a trolley passing, people talking, a horse neighing, a horn sounding, each detached, immovable, separated from its source, without meaning. Around me, the other children, heads bent over their work, were robots or puppets, moved by an invisible mechanism. On the platform, the teacher, too, talking, gesticulating, rising to write on the blackboard, was a grotesque jack-in-the-box. And always this ghastly quiet, broken by outside sounds coming from far away, the implacable sun heating the room, the lifeless immobility. An awful terror bound me; I wanted to scream.

On the way to school in the morning at seven-thirty, sometimes the same thing happened. Suddenly the street became infinite, white under the brilliant sun; people ran about like ants on an ant-hill; automobiles circled in all directions aimlessly; in the distance a bell pealed. Then everything seemed to stop, to wait, to hold its breath, in a state of extreme tension, the tension of the needle in the haystack. Something seemed about to occur, some extraordinary catastophe. An overpowering anxiety forced me to stop and wait. Then, without anything having actually changed, again realizing the senseless activity of people and things, I went on my way to school.

Happily for me, I fell ill with pulmonary tuberculosis and had to leave school at once for a mountain sanatorium. There, after a few days of anxiety due to the change, I made a ready adjustment because of the regularity of the life.

The crises of unreality decreased noticeably, to be replaced by states of fervor, of exaltation over nature. I was alone in a small room. To listen to the autumn wind rushing through the woods was my greatest joy. But the shrieking and groaning of the forest treated thus roughly aroused an uneasiness that spoiled the pleasure. I believed the wind blew from the North Pole, traveling over the icy Siberian steppes, moaning and protesting in the forest; it was alive, monstrous, bending everything in its way. Then my room became enormous, disproportionate, the walls smooth and shining, the glaring electric light bathing everything in its blinding brightness. The violence of the wind outside rattling the blinds, the rustling, the strangled sighs of the pine branches bowing under the wind, furnished a striking contrast to the quiet and immobility within. Again the terror mounted to a paroxysm. Desperately I wanted to break the circle of unreality which froze me in the midst of this electric immobility.

When we were not engaged in treatment, I asked a friend to play or to talk to me. But despite the play and the conversation, I could not get back to reality. Everything looked artificial, mechanical, electric. To get rid of it I tried to rouse myself. I laughed, I jumped, I pushed things around, shook them to make them come to life. These were horribly painful moments.

How relieved I was when things remained in their customary framework, when people were alive and normal and especially when I had contact with them!

I came down from the mountain for three months, only to go up again for a full year. It was during this year, the first of January to be exact, that for the first time I felt *real fear*. I should emphasize that the unreality had grown greater and the wind had taken on a specific meaning. On windy days in bad weather I was horribly upset. At night I could not sleep, listening to the wind, sharing its howls, its complaints and despairing cries, and my soul wept and groaned with it. More and more I imagined the wind bore a message for me to divine. But what? I still did not know.

It was New Year's when I first experienced what I called *Fear*. It literally fell on me, how I know not. It was afternoon, the wind was stronger than ever and more mournful. I was in the mood to listen to it, my whole being attuned to it, palpitating, awaiting I know not what. Suddenly Fear, agonizing, boundless Fear, overcame me, not the usual uneasiness of unreality, but real fear, such as one knows at the approach of danger, of calamity. And the wind, as if to add to the turmoil, soughed its interminable protests, echoing the muffled groans of the forest.

Fear made me ill; just the same I ran out to visit a friend who was staying at a nearby sanatorium. To get there, a way led through the woods, short and well-marked. Becoming lost in the thick fog, I circled round and round the sanatorium without seeing it, my fear augmenting all the while. By and by I realized that the wind inspired this fear; the trees too, large and black in the mist, but particularly the wind. At length I grasped the meaning of its message: the frozen wind from the North Pole wanted to crush the earth, to destroy it. Or perhaps it was an omen, a sign that the earth was about to be laid waste. This idea tormented me with growing intensity. But I remained unaware of the basis for the fear which from then on came over me at any moment of the day.

I told the doctor about it. He wanted to help me by hypnosis, but not wanting to lose control of my own personality; I fought vehemently against it, preferring to endure both the fear and the cries of unreality.

Outwardly, however, no one suspected the inquietude or the fear. People thought I was hysterical or manic. Actually, I was indeed always agitated, cutting capers, laughing at the top of my voice, playing the fool. Yet these symptoms were not those of an excited girl, unable to control herself, but an attempt to master the fear, which, when it came over me, made me agitated, anxious, waiting imminent misfortune. I sought distraction in games and conversation but soon the fear grew again and the help I hoped to find in my friends proved of no avail. Then I tried to flee the fear in excitement. I shouted and laughed, as an escape from the fear and a defense against it.

Little by little I brought myself to confide to my friends that the world was about to be destroyed, that planes were coming to bomb and annihilate us. Although I often offered these confidences jestingly I firmly believed them and, to feel less alone, I wanted to share the fears with others. Nonetheless, I did not believe the world would be destroyed as I believed in real facts. Vaguely I had some misgivings that this belief was linked to my own personal fear, that it was specific and not generally held.

So I passed a year, suffering the fear and unreality. Except for these manic periods, I was myself. The children in the hospital were fond of me and treated me like a little mother. I read them the letters they received and wrote for the little ones.

I returned to the valley, physically recovered, but with worse morale. Now I had to reckon with "the Fear" which abruptly overcame me and robbed me of all joy in living. In addition, the difficulty of readjustment to family and school life was incredible.

Just the same I was a good student. Drawing, sewing and singing remained weak subjects. Concluding my efforts were in vain, I hardly tried to understand perspective, rhythm, or the placing of fabric; I had completely lost the sense of perspective.

The two years preceding psychoanalysis were years of struggle and incessant exertion. Beneath the exterior of a girl, hardworking and full of responsibility (I managed a household of six persons on a pitiful budget, educated my brothers and sisters, and was an excellent student), I felt more and more bewildered. The Fear, previously episodic, now never left me. Every day I was sure to sense it, and the unreal situations increased as well. Until quite recently, the feeling of unreality had involved only things, but with people I knew I had maintained contact.

Since the return from the mountains, unreality had crept over people, even friends. It was a torment. There were two or three girls, ten years or so older than I, whom I used to see each week. They complained that I was clinging and demanding, for when one of them suggested an hour's walk, at the moment of parting I implored her to stay with me for a little while, to come back with me. And when she acceded to my wish, I was still not satisfied: "Not yet, not yet; please stay with me." These incessant protests made me seem ungrateful and insistent, but they were due to the unreal state I was in.

During the visit I tried to establish contact with her, to feel that she was actually there, alive and sensitive. But it was futile. Though I certainly recognized her, she became part of the unreal world. I knew her name and everything about her, yet she appeared strange, unreal, like a statue. I saw her eyes, her nose, her lips moving, heard her voice and understood what she said perfectly, yet I was in the presence of a stranger. To restore contact between us I made desperate efforts to break through the invisible dividing wall but the harder I tried, the less successful I was, and the uneasiness grew apace.

We were walking on a country road, chatting as two friends do. I was telling her what went on at school, my triumphs and failures; I spoke of my brothers and sisters, sometimes of my troubles. And beneath this mask of tranquillity, of normality, I was living a veritable drama. Around us the fields spread away, cut up by hedges or clumps of trees, the white road ran ahead of us, the sun shone in the blue sky and warmed our backs. But I saw a boundless plain, unlimited, the horizon infinite. The trees and hedges were of cardboard, placed here and there, like stage accessories, and the road, oh, the endless road, white, glittering under the sun's rays, glittering like a needle, above us the remorseless sun weighing down trees and houses under its electric rays. Over and above the vastness reigned a terrifying quiet, broken by noises making the silence still more quiet and terrifying. And I—I was lost with my friend in the limitless space.

But is it really she, this woman who is speaking, gesticulating? I see her shining white teeth, her brown eyes looking at me. And I perceive a statue by my side, a puppet, part of the pasteboard scenery. What fear, what anguish! I say to her, "Jean, is it really you?" And she answers, amazed, "Who do you think it is; you know very well it is I, don't you?" "Oh, yes, yes; I know perfectly well it is you." But to myself I say, "Yes, it is she, but disguised." I continue, "Why do you behave like an automaton?" "Oh," she replies, offended, "you think I walk awkwardly, but it's not my fault."

My friend has not understood the question. I keep quiet, more alone and isolated than ever. Then comes the time to go our separate ways. The anxiety exacerbates. At any price, by any means, I must conquer this unreality, for an instant feel someone alive near me, experience for a second the life-giving contact that makes up in a moment for the loneliness of a day. I lean on my friend's arm and implore her to stay a few minutes more. If she agrees to my request, I talk, I ask questions, with the sole objective of breaking through the barrier between us. But time passes and I am no further. So I accompany her a little way, waiting, hoping that a miracle will restore reality, life, sensibility. I look at her, study her, praying to feel the life in her through the enveloping unreality. But she seems more a statue than ever, a mannikin moved by a mechanism, talking like an automaton. It is horrible, inhuman, grotesque. Defeated, offering conventional goodbyes, I leave, exhausted, deathly sad. With heart empty, despairingly empty, I reach home. There I find a pasteboard house, sisters and brothers robots, the electric light—I am plunged into the nightmare of the needle in the hay. In this aura I make dinner, coach the children in their homework and do my own tasks.

Sometimes, thanks to the customary preparations and to the warmth and taste of food, reality is restored. So great is the joy, so precious the sense of well-being, doled out to me sparingly, stingily, that I do not want to go to bed.

Riquette

[Renee, who had never cared for dolls, suddenly, at the age of seventeen or eighteen, began to play with them like a little girl. This, objectively, indicates a regression due to the development of the disease (a process described in *La réalisation symbolique,* page 17). But what does the doll represent to Renee? This is what she says.]

3 While I was at the sanatorium, by mistake (I was fifteen and a half years old) I was given a gift of a large and beautiful doll for New Year's. Feeling quite frustrated, I decided to send it to my two little sisters but I couldn't find a box big enough. So I kept the doll and put it in the children's dormitory on a couch in a large bay window. Though completely without interest in it, nevertheless any time the window was opened—it was midwinter—I felt slightly uneasy and guilty that the doll was left uncovered. I was ashamed of the feeling, and in order not to feel obliged to cover her, I had to turn my eyes away any time I entered the room.

It was shortly after returning to the valley that I began to concern myself with Riquette. The period was a difficult one; I could not make the adjustment to life at home and to school responsibilities. I longed for the mountains, for the well-ordered, automatic life at the sanatorium, a life without demands.

One day while I was cleaning my sisters' rooms, I noticed in a pile of old material a stuffed doll with a painted face, discolored and smeared, the frizzled wool hair redbrown, the whole body dirty from being dragged on the floor.

Obedient to an unconscious inpulse, I pulled the doll out of the rags and laid her in a carriage, replacing Lily, a comparatively beautiful porcelain doll. When my eight year old sister saw the exchange and asked me why, I answered that Riquette needed the carriage for sun treatments. My little sister had loved Riquette before Lily and she accepted the explanation. From that day the carriage and Riquette were my property.

Each afternoon before leaving for school, I drew the carriage to the open window and at great length studied how Riquette could avoid the sun on her head during my absence. At four o'clock I ran home, out of breath, to throw a little doll's dress over the bathing suit and to let her sit up for a while. At night, I spent much time covering her and tucking her in. During the winter I spent hours devising the best way for her to be warm enough without perspiring, to benefit from the cold air without getting sick. Oddly, the problem of feeding her did not concern me at all. Only her physical, or sensory, well-being—position, heat, cold, light, humidity—interested me. Sometimes, though, I wheeled the little carriage into the kitchen so that Riquette should not feel lonely.

At times, during more lucid moments, I was frightened at the importance she had in my life, particularly when my brothers and sisters made fun of a very real solicitude. They were astonished that, loving her as I seemed to, I didn't make any clothes for her. But this was because my love for Riquette was very one-sided, and was concerned only with temperatures. To every other consideration of appearance, of cleanliness, of feeding, I was completely indifferent.

For me this doll *"really"* existed, but the existence was purely affective. When, for instance, I forgot to cover her more warmly toward evening, I dropped the things I was doing and rushed to her, examining her, rubbing her to restore warmth. Sometimes my little sister observed, "If you've forgotten to cover her, what of it? You know perfectly well she isn't alive and doesn't feel anything!" I was stupefied at her remark, but it did not alter the actuality of my concern. Often this servitude weighed heavily and I should have liked to become indifferent to Riquette and occupy myself no more with her. But this did not happen. Just the same I did not believe that she was really alive, since I never gave her anything to eat.

For me, she represented the ideal of an infant's happiness: to be always exactly at the most physiologically agreeable temperature, placed in the most relaxing position where the body feels best. I should have liked to place her in a knee-bent position but her legs were stiff and this was impossible. I showed her my love solely on the level of physiological well-being.

I Go into Psychoanalysis
and Find a Mama

4 The first two years of analysis were combatting the Fear and the Enlightenment. It was a titanic struggle and I was weak and disabled in the face of what I called the "Land of Light."

During the earliest attacks of Fear and an intense unreality, I sometimes uttered these unconscious and shocking words: "I should prefer to escape into madness to avoid this consuming Fear." Alas, I did not know what I was saying. In my ignorance I believed that madness was a state of insensibility where there was neither pain nor suffering nor joy, but particularly, no responsibility. Never, not for an instant, had I even imagined what "to lose one's reason" actually meant. And now I was in the midst of fighting desperately not to slip into it, not to be submerged in the "electric light."

It was in the course of the first year of analysis that I realized the danger I was in. For me, madness was definitely not a condition of illness; I did not believe that I was ill. It was rather a country, opposed to Reality, where reigned an implacable light, blinding, leaving no place for shadow; an immense space without boundary, limitless, flat; a mineral, lunar country, cold as the wastes of the North Pole. In this stretching emptiness, all is unchangeable, immobile, congealed, crystallized. Objects are stage trappings, placed here and there, geometric cubes without meaning.

People turn weirdly about, they make gestures, movements without sense; they are phantoms whirling on an infinite plain, crushed by the pitiless electric light. And I— I am lost in it, isolated, cold, stripped, purposeless under the light. A wall of brass separates me from everybody and everything. In the midst of desolation, in indescribable distress, in absolute solitude, I am terrifyingly alone; no one comes to help me. This was it; this was madness, the Enlightenment was the perception of Unreality. Madness was finding oneself permanently in an all-embracing Unreality. I called it the

"Land of Light" because of the brilliant illumination, dazzling, astral, cold, and the state of extreme tension in which everything was, including myself. It was as if an electric current of extraordinary power ran through every object, building until the whole blew up in a frightful explosion.

This is why I complained to the analyst of the "Straw" and why I could not draw the "Little Personage" without adding a "Straw," that is a narrow wire passing through the body, or rather through the mind, representing the tension of unreality and at the same time recalling the nightmare of the needle in the haystack. For this reason I called it "the Straw" as a reminder of the hay.

In the endless silence and the strained immobility, I had the impression that some dreadful thing about to occur would break the quiet, something horrible, overwhelming. I waited, holding my breath, suffused with inquietude, but nothing happened. The immobility became more immobile, the silence more silent, things and people, their gestures and their noises, more artificial, detached one from the other, unreal, without life. And my fear increased, became inexpressible, shattering, intolerable.

Against this enlightenment I waged a battle with the help of the analyst who later became my "Mama." Only near her I felt secure, especially from the time when she began to sit next to me on the couch and put her arm around my shoulders. Oh, what joy, what relief to feel the life, the warmth, the reality! From the moment I left her at the end of the session, I began to count the hours and the minutes: only twenty-four hours, only twenty-three and a half hours, only eighteen hours.

Alas this happiness, this little island of reality was soon to be taken from me. Indeed, I saw Mama's face become cold, cut out of cardboard, unreal. Despite my frantic, violent need to "feel" her, to have contact with her—the only contact remaining to me —I saw that little by little she became part of the Enlightenment. Then I said to her, "You disguise yourself to punish me." At times, swayed by her denials and thanks to her affection—particularly when she held me close against her—and when she said, "But Mama is always the same. She is stronger than the 'Enlightenment'; notice how firmly she holds you," then I recognized her, she was again herself, my refuge, my life, my very reality, the precious little oasis of reality in the desert world of my soul.

I Enter the System

5 Very soon after the beginning of analysis I understood that my fear was a cover for guilt, a guilt infinite and awful. During the early sessions, masturbation and the hostility I harbored toward everyone seemed to lie at the bottom. I literally hated people, without knowing why. In dreams and frequently in waking fantasies I constructed an electric machine to blow up the earth and everyone with it. But what was even worse, with the machine I would rob all men of their brains, thus creating robots obedient to my will alone. This was my greatest, most terrible revenge.

Later, considering them appropriate, I no longer felt guilty about these fantasies, nor did the guilt have an actual object. It was too pervasive, and it demanded punishment. The punishment was indeed horrible, sadistic—it consisted, fittingly enough, of being guilty. For to feel oneself guilty is the worst that can happen, it is the punishment of punishments. Consequently, I could never be relieved of it as though I had been truly punished. Quite the reverse, I felt more and more guilty, immeasurably guilty. Constantly, I sought to discover what was punishing me so dreadfully, what was making me so guilty.

One day I wrote a letter of entreaty to the unknown author of my suffering, to the Persecutor, asking him to tell me what evil I had done, that I might finally know. But because I did not know where to send my letter, I tore it up.

Some time after I discovered that the Persecutor was none other than the electric machine, that is, it was the "System" that was punishing me. I thought of it as some vast world-like entity encompassing all men. At the top were those who gave orders, who imposed punishment, who pronounced others guilty. But they were themselves guilty. Since every man was responsible for all other men, each of his acts had a repercussion on other beings. A formidable interdependence bound all men under the scourge of culpability. Everyone was part of the

System. But only some were aware of being part.

They were the ones who were "Enlightened" (see footnote, page 24) as I was. And it was the same time both an honor and a misfortune to have this awareness. Those who were not part of it—though actually, of course, they were—were unaware of the System. As a result, they felt not at all guilty, and I envied them intensely.

At this moment, the ring closed: the Land of Enlightenment was the same as the System. That is why to enter into it was to become insensible of everything except culpability, the supreme punishment, freely granted by the System. I was guilty, abominably, intolerably guilty, without cause and without motive. Any punishment, the very worst, could be imposed on me—it would never deliver me of the load. Because, as I have already said, the most dreadful punishment was to make me feel eternally, universally culpable.

It was only when I was near "Mama," my analyst, that I felt a little better. But even for this, nearly an hour had to go by. Indeed, it was only toward the end of the hour, and sometimes not until twenty minutes after it, that I made contact with "Mama." When I arrived, I was as if frozen. I saw the room, the furniture, "Mama" herself, each thing separate, detached from the others, cold, implacable, inhuman, by dint of being without life. Then I began to relate what had happened since the last visit and relived it in the telling. But the sound of my voice and the meaning of my words seemed strange. Every now and then, an inner voice interrupted sneeringly, "Ah, Ah!" and mockingly repeated what I had said.

These inner voices had the aspect of the needle in the hay. They were affected, ridiculous. "Ah, ah! then the teacher said, said," and the voices dwelt stiltedly on "said, said," I struggled to repress them, to pay no attention. But they would not obey, the mocking reptitions continued. Often images were associated with the phrases. For example, if I wanted to recount that my German teacher had made some remark or that my little sister had made a row over going to school, I saw the German teacher gesticulating at his desk like a puppet, separated from everything, alone under a blinding light, waving his arms like a maniac. And I saw my little sister, rolling on the kitchen floor in a rage; but she too was changed by some mechanism, apparently purposeless.

These people who in reality behaved in accordance with goals and well-defined incentives became void and lost their souls. Only their bodies were left them, moving like automatons, and their movements were deprived of emotions and feelings. This was awful. To get rid of these images, of these inner voices, I looked at "Mama." But I perceived a statue, a figure of ice which smiled at me. And this smile, showing her white teeth, frightened me. For I saw the individual features of her face, separated from each other: the teeth, then the nose, then the cheeks, then one eye and the other. Perhaps it was this independence of each part that inspired such fear and prevented my recognizing her even though I knew who she was.

In the rest of the room, in the silence, everything was there, posed, congealed, stupid. And the terror, the mad anguish, mounted in me. I hid myself against Mama's shoulder, shielded my arm, feeling her warmth and the faint fragrance on her clothes. I closed my eyes and cried, "I'm afraid, I'm afraid, the straw is there, and you don't exist. Help me, help me, the System is going to get me, the waters are rising. I am going to drown, I am cold, I am plunged in cold; oh, how afraid I am; why have you changed, why have you become a statue and let the System give you orders, oh! why?"

I clung desperately to her, clutching at her dress. I wanted to take refuge in her, to hide in her heart, to escape the frightful anguish that overwhelmed me.

All this time I heard the mocking sneers and the stilted unrelated phrases repeating, "And we shall see," or "Battle of Trafalgar," or "Yes, miss."

Then Mama's sweet voice sounded in the midst of this madness and she was saying, "Little Renee, my little Renee needn't be afraid when there is a Mama. Renee is not alone now. Mama is here to take care of her. She is stronger than everything else, stronger than the 'Enlightenment.' Mama will take Renee out of the water; we will win. See how strong Mama is, she knows how to protect Renee. Renee has nothing to fear." And she passed her light hand over my head and kissed my forehead. Then, her voice, the caress on my hair, her protection, began to exert their charm.

Little by little, the phrases and sneers disappeared, the unreal perception of the room no longer mattered; I closed my eyes. What did me the most amazing good was her use of the third person in speaking of herself, "Mama and Renee," not "I and you." When by chance she used the first person, abruptly I no longer knew her, and I was angry that she had, by this error, broken my contact with her. So that when she said, "You will see how together we shall fight against the System," (what were "I" and "you?") for me there was no reality. Only "Mama,"

"Renee," or, better still, "the little personage," contained reality, life, affectivity.

I did not know how to explain to Mama all that went on. I believed that she understood anyway. So when I complained of these distressing experiences in such words as "I am afraid," or "the straw is spreading," or "everything is separated," or "you are disguised as ice," or "it is cold," wonderfully enough, Mama divined the horror.

Sometimes when I told her "The phrases are playing tricks on me and making fun of me," Mama chased them away, saying, "Renee should listen only to Mama's voice; it is important, for Mama's voice loves Renee." Then I heard this marvelous voice which, like a talisman, could give me again a moment of reality, a contact with life. Relieved, but exhausted by the struggle and anxiety, I began to talk a little of what absorbed and interested me. But, alas, it was already time to leave.

Warmed again, encouraged, softly repeating Mama's words, I went home. Once in the street, however, I saw again the pasteboard scenery of unreality. Nevertheless, I did not suffer from it as I had at the beginning of the session for I still kept a little of Mama's warmth, her words in my heart. Particularly, I no longer struggled to break the unreality but submitted to the old perception without trying to change it. As for the way home, the people, or the objects I passed, I experienced no further pressing need to enter into contact with them as with Mama.

I was glad that Mama changed her method at the end of the first year of analysis. In the beginning, she analyzed everything I said, my fear, my guilt. These investigations seemed to me like a bill of complaints, quite as though in looking for the cause of feelings, they became more at fault and more real. As if to say, "Find out in what instances you are guilty, and why." This for me was proof that the guilt existed, that the System was really there since one could find the reason for its actions. From these sessions I went home more unhappy, more blameworthy, more isolated than ever, without any contact, alone in my own unreal world.

But after Mama sat down beside me, talked to me in the third person and especially seemed to understand without looking for causes at all, how relieved I was! She alone could break through the unreal wall that hemmed me in; she alone kept me in some contact with life.

The System Gives Me Orders and Things Begin to Come to Life

6 Unreality finally reached such a point that Mama herself could no longer make contact between us. For some time I had been complaining bitterly that things were tricking me and how I suffered because of it.

As a matter of fact, these "things" weren't doing anything special; they didn't speak, nor attack me directly. It was their very presence that made me complain. I saw things, smooth as metal, so cut off, so detached from each other, so illuminated and tense that they filled me with terror. When, for example, I looked at a chair or a jug, I thought not of their use or function—a jug not as something to hold water and milk, a chair not as something to sit in—but as having lost their names, their functions and meanings; they became "things" and began to take on life, to exist.

This existence accounted for my great fear. In the unreal scene, in the murky quiet of my perception, suddenly "the thing" sprang up. The stone jar, decorated with blue flowers, was there facing me, defying me with its presence, with its existence. To conquer my fear I looked away. My eyes met a chair, then a table; they were alive, too, asserting their presence. I attempted to escape their hold by calling out their names. I said, "chair, jug, table, it is a chair." But the word echoed hollowly, deprived of all meaning; it had left the object, was divorced from it, so much so that on one hand it was a living, mocking thing, on the other, a name, robbed of sense, an envelope emptied of content. Nor was I able to bring the two together, but stood rooted there before them, filled with fear and impotence.

When I protested, "Things are tricking me; I am afraid," and people asked specifically, "Do you see the jug and the chair as alive?" I answered, "Yes, they are alive." And they, the doctors, too, thought I saw these things as humans whom I heard speak. But it was not that. Their life consisted uniquely in the fact that they were there, in their existence itself.

To flee from them I hid my head in my hands or stood in a corner. I lived through a period of intense suffering. Everything was alive, defied me. Outside in the street people were struck mad, moved around without reason, encountered each other and things which had become more real than they.

At the same time I received orders from the System. I did not hear the orders as voices; yet they were as imperious as if uttered in a loud voice. While, for example, I was preparing to do some typing, suddenly, without any warning a force, which was not an impulse but rather resembled a command, ordered me to burn my right hand or the building in which I was. With all my strength I resisted the order, I telephoned Mama to tell her about it. Her voice, urging me to listen to her and not to the System, reassured me. If the System became too demanding I was to run to her. This calmed me considerably, but unfortunately only for a moment.

An indescribable anguish squeezed my heart, an anguish no resolve could allay. If I refused to obey, I felt guilty and cowardly for not daring, and the anguish mounted. Then the order became more insistent. If, finally to obey, I went to the fire and stretched out my hand, an intense feeling of guilt overcame me as though I were doing something wicked, and the anxiety waxed in proportion. I should say, however, that the latter alternative provoked the greater disturbance, for I felt that if I obeyed the order, I should commit an act irreparably damaging to my personality. And yet in both cases, obedience or disobedience, was something artificial, something theatrical. Meanwhile, I was alone; no one except Mama knew of my battle.

I had, too, the conviction that my behavior was deceitful. In reality, it wasn't anything of the kind. I was deeply sincere. But if I disobeyed the System to maintain the integrity of my personality, I was deceitful since I acted as though I had no consideration for the order. If I obeyed it, I was equally deceitful, since I did not agree to burn myself. I suffered horribly from the orders and from the feeling of treachery so contrary to my character.

While I fought with all my strength not to let myself sink in the Enlightenment, I saw things mocking me from their places, taunting me threateningly. And in my head foolish phrases floated around without letup. I closed my eyes to escape the surrounding turmoil of which I was the center. But I could find no rest, for horrible images assailed me, so vivid that I experienced actual physical sensation. I cannot say that

I really saw images; they did not represent anything. Rather I felt them. It seemed that my mouth was full of birds which I crunched between my teeth, and their feathers, their blood and broken bones were choking me. Or I saw people whom I had entombed in milk bottles, putrefying, and I was consuming their rotting cadavers. Or I was devouring the head of a cat which meanwhile gnawed at my vitals. It was ghastly, intolerable.

In the midst of this horror and turbulence, I nonetheless carried on my work as a secretary. But with what hardship! Adding to the torment, strident noises, piercing cries began to hammer in my head. Their unexpectedness made me jump. Nonetheless, I did not hear them as I heard real cries uttered by real people. The noises, localized on the right side, drove me to stop up my ears. But I readily distinguished them from the noises of reality. I heard them without hearing them, and recognized that they arose within me.

I knew that more and more I would let myself be controlled by the System, that I would sink down in the Land of Enlightenment, or the Land of Commandment, as I also called it.

My only moments of peace were the analytic sessions, particularly toward the end of the hour when I had finally secured some contact with Mama. I implored her to save me from the clutches of the Enlightenment and the animation of Things.

But despite her good intentions, she was then powerless against the System. That she was able to resist it and that I could always run back to her when I was in danger was in itself a remarkable victory.

At last the tragedy occurred.* The orders became more imperious, more demanding. I was to burn my right hand, for the right hand was the hand of the law.

In the System a formidable interdependence existed. Without knowing it, I had ordered that people be punished, and in my turn, I was to be punished. Those who had received punishment from me had the right to punish, but for each punishment they meted out, one was incurred. When I understood the mechanism of the System of Punishments which engulfed me, I fought less and less against the orders.

One day, trembling, I placed the back of my right hand on the incandescent coals and held it there as long as possible. By thinking of my duty to the System, and that it might then stop issuing injunctions, I was able to stand the pain. At this moment the head of

* The analyst was in close contact with the psychiatrist who occasionally saw Renee. In view of her mother's opposition, he could not hospitalize her without a provocative incident.

the office came in unexpectedly. Quickly withdrawing my hand, I was relieved at the thought that he had not seen me. But I was mistaken. He had no doubt grasped the situation at once, for he notified the physician of the Council for Supervision of the Mentally Ill, who happened to be my own doctor.

Realizing their intention of hospitalizing me after consultation, I spoke of the objects making fun of me and of the System surrounding me, since these had become a part of me, but I kept quiet about the burn and the orders I had received, for I had never been altogether in agreement with them. However, that was enough to prompt hospitalization, lest, without it, I be officially committed to an institution.

I Am Hospitalized; the System Persists and I Risk Losing Mama

7 The necessity of entering a hospital for mental cases, or any hospital for that matter, was extremely disturbing. Just the same I was grateful not to be forcibly committed as could easily have been the case. In this connection something extraordinary happened, something unique in my life.

From the time the System's orders first assailed me I was in constant fear of entering altogether into the Land of Enlightenment. Theoretically this meant remaining forever in unreality without any contact with Mama; practically it meant being shut up in a hospital. I comprehended perfectly the relation between the Land of Enlightenment and the state of madness. To me the mentally ill were the "enlightened" ones and to enter a psychiatric institution was to be completely "enlightened." Often I said to Mama, "I'm afraid; they're coming to get me to put me with the 'enlightened ones.'"

Indeed, ten days after the visit of the physician from the Council of Supervision, they actually came to my home in a taxi to commit me officially, a nurse and a social worker or woman police officer. Fortunately, for me I was out and my family did not know where I was. It was a late Saturday afternoon about six o'clock, a day when I had by chance accompanied Mama to a lecture after the analytic session. Oddly, a strange disturbance had come over me during the lecture and I said to Mama, "The hospital warden is there, he has just come for me! I'm afraid, I'm afraid, protect me, I implore you!" and I repeated these words several times. I had not seen the warden but I had a premonition of imminent peril. In reality, I was quite unaware of what was brewing in my case, and far from any certainty that they wanted to hospitalize me, especially that day.

Mama comforted me and I left her reassured. I started for home, which was about a half hour's walk from the lecture hall and from Mama's office, going at a good clip because of the usual Saturday tasks waiting for me at home. Suddenly I stopped. Without any anxiety, without any intention of being dramatic, and moved by some unseen force, I turned around and went back to Mama. When she opened the door she was quite astonished to see me. It was the first time I had ever returned once I had left her. Telling her what had come over me halfway home, I suddenly added, "I came back so that you would protect me from the warden. He wants to take me."

I was a little embarrassed to bother Mama without a real and pressing cause, the more that the anxiety during the lecture had now vanished. Needless to say, Mama welcomed me and kept me for over an hour. Then I left and went home where, to my surprise, I found the atmosphere extremely tense. I asked them what had happened and in answer to my insistent questions, my brothers told me the story. "A male nurse (the warden) and a welfare worker had come to fetch me in the hospital ambulance by order of the Council of Supervision." The time of their arrival coincided with the end of the lecture when I had had the foreboding of their coming and had communicated as much to Mama. It seems that they had waited an hour and a half; had I not had the remarkable inspiration to turn back when I was half way home, I should have arrived early and been taken by force. Thanks to it, however, I had escaped an almost irremediable shock. Finally, tired of waiting and not knowing when I might return, they had left.

As it worked out, Mama had time to arrange the matter so that I could enter a private voluntary hospital with open wards.

At first I felt considerable relief in this refuge, sheltered from the orders of the System, for I was not allowed in the kitchen or in any place where there was fire or matches. Nonetheless the orders became more frequent and soon I felt compelled to do everything in my power to carry them out. I tried to get to the kitchen for matches or to burn myself on the stove. Gas had no interest for me, for according to the System, its flame, made artificially by man, was impure. But a nurse always followed me the moment she saw me leave the lounge or my own room and prevented my entering the kitchen.

How relieved I was when I realized how altogether impossible it was to carry out the orders! For I was still well enough to feel—if not to understand—that obedience to the System's orders involved severe damage to the integrity of my personality. When, then, the nurse placed an obstacle in the way I no longer had to struggle against them.

I had observed that if I acceded to the

orders, the System, instead of leaving me alone, became on the contrary more demanding. Furthermore, if I was allowed to reach the kitchen, the impulse became more urgent and I was literally torn in two. On one hand, my intelligence clung to the System and believed absolutely in its reality and its power; on the other hand, a dim, indescribable presentiment, an instinct of self-preservation, was aroused and held me back each time I was ordered to burn myself. The same dilemma was unresolved in my conscience; I felt guilty in struggling against the orders, guilty in obeying them.

It was because of this dilemma that only a material obstacle freed me of the conflict. When I was moved by the impulse to burn myself, I went downstairs and hurried to the kitchen. Sometimes, if I found it locked, I waited at the door; then, since there was nothing else to do, went back to my room. Most of the time, though, I stood frozen at the door, unable to leave despite a numbing weariness and I was happy when the nurse took me by the arm and led me away.

Unfortunately the director of the hospital was much interested in psychological abnormalties (something I learned later when I was well) and, when she saw me going to the kitchen, instead of barring my way, pretended not to notice, and let me carry out my impulse. Following very quietly, she observed what I was going to do, yet she allowed me to reach my objective and only interfered at the last moment when I reached toward the flame or the match box.

Sometimes I sensed her behind me and hated her for letting me struggle alone against the impulse to carry out the order, a struggle moreover in which I was always vanquished. Because of the anxiety it aroused and the state of unreality in which I found myself, this constant combat was especially wearing and added to the increasing severity of the orders. Since each time I was deterred by an outside obstacle the orders became more infrequent, the director's behavior caused me a great deal of harm.

The orders grew in intensity and the doctor could no longer keep me in an open hospital and had me transferred to an institute with locked wards. Frightful anguish seized me at the thought of entering a hospital for "enlightened people." It seemed that my ultimate entrance into the "Land of Enlightenment" was sealed. Weeping, I implored them to keep me and I promised not to obey the System. But it was to no avail; I was to leave. My promises certainly were of no value; I was incapable of keeping them. Nonetheless I knew that if I did not require constant watching they would let me stay. Yet, despite the conviction and particularly despite the intense desire to remain near Geneva where Mama could see me every day, and despite my awful fear of being shut up in the "Hospital for Enlightened People," I could not bring myself to disobey the System's orders. On the contrary, under the influence of my wish to see them decrease, they seemed perversely to augment.

At length the dreadful day arrived. They came for me by car and my nurse went with me. It was understood that I was to enter a private hospital adjoining a cantonal asylum some distance from Geneva. Unluckily, by mistake I was taken, not to the private hospital, but to the locked female ward of the asylum. When they pushed me into the observation room and I saw the great bars on the windows, the screaming women, complaining or transfixed in odd poses, motionless as statues, I knew that I should die of anguish. Without so much as a good-bye, my nurse had disappeared. I remained alone in the midst of this fantastic setting, crushed by terror and paralyzing despair.

A nurse led me to the bathroom, helped me undress, slipped a big gown of rough material over me and made me get into a nearby cold bath. I shook with cold, with weariness and terror, like a bird fallen from the nest, surrounded by mortal danger.

But deep within me, without suspecting it, a defense was organizing against what had befallen me. I did not weep as I wished to do, nor was I silent. The first words I uttered after my arrival was a reasonable request that a little warm water be added to the bath. When the nurse refused, I assured her that I had just been ill with lung trouble and was consequently very delicate, and that I would probably catch cold, particularly with the windows open in midwinter. These protestations represented the early form of the defense building up in me. Actually, I was not at all in the habit of complaining, certainly not about the cold. On the contrary, I, who was ordinarily quite Spartan, was astonished now at my own concern at catching cold.

Not until an hour and a half later was I permitted to get out of the bath and go back to the observation room where my bed was placed between two other girls and opposite the beds of three other women. On my side, the girls were patients in the private hospital but were too ill to remain on its semi-open wards; facing us were poor patients committed there by the canton.

I remained lying on my back, rigid, in a position of tense resistance, watching everything around me, trying to concentrate both physically and mentally on what was going on in the room. In my heart was horror, confusion, indescribable anxiety, endless despair. A ceaseless voice within me repeated over and over, "This is it, Renee, this is what the System has done to you! You see, Renee, it has locked you up in the Land of Enlightenment. You are alone in your punishment. I am alone and afraid. Renee is afraid."

With all my strength I tried to choke off the poor little voice, this baby's voice speaking in the third person like a tiny child. At all costs I must quiet it, hear it no more, for should it persist in its complaints in the little incessantly repeated phrases, I was certain that the bastions of my defense would crumble and I would scream in grief and anguish.

I looked wildly around me, then, feeling that I was about to be vanquished in the struggle, I took up the knitting I had brought with me and began feverishly to work on some baby booties, concentrating desperately on counting stitches. But the little voice continued more firmly: "Mama, Renee is afraid; the System has punished Renee; Renee is afraid."

Fortunately, a patient came over to my bed and delivered a lecture much of which was given over to sex. Then a woman doctor made rounds. She asked me a lot of questions but instinctively I said nothing of the System nor of the orders and very carefully spoke at length about a great many things of no importance at all. I remarked that she resembled a friend of mine whom I found very pretty. I asked her when I could leave this room, that I wanted a room of my own, no matter what, even were it in the basement or a little cell.

To this she replied that there were no available rooms in that section and that I would be transferred to the private hospital when I no longer received orders. Then I, who was ordinarily markedly taciturn, was suddenly deluged in a flood of my own words, talking, talking, interrupting the nurses. And I continued to knit. Yet this tireless activity could not altogether stifle the little voice. The effort that I was making to control my anxiety and fear was so intense that I perspired profusely, even though it was midwinter.

In addition to this, I was too afraid of the other patients the first night to close my eyes and the following nights I woke at every sound. Then, too, it was impossible to sleep with the cries and complaints of the two women occupying cells off the observation room.

The nurse on duty assured me that I had nothing to fear from the other patients. Just the same, the moment she was gone, the woman in the bed opposite got up, ran toward my bed, snatched the apples and pears on my night table, took refuge in her own bed and swallowed the fruit almost at a gulp. This frightened me, and when the nurse returned I told her what had happened.

She looked at me sternly and said, "Miss, you mustn't begin by telling lies; that doesn't go around here. What you say is impossible. That woman has refused to eat for three years and requires artificial feeding." And when I insisted, "Now, now, stop your lying or I'll tell the doctor." And she left.

I was quite cast down, wondering whether I had dreamed this story of the theft. Never in my life had I been accused of lying. That evening, however, while arranging the patient, the nurse found the stems and the pear pits and a half-eaten apple. Turning to me she laughed and said, without a word of excuse, "It was true!" When the physician making rounds heard the story she was highly amused. "That's a good way to get Mrs. X to eat. From now on, we will put food on Miss Renee's night table and Mrs. X will go and take it!" And my fear grew more lively.

The next day a big woman came toward me from her cell and said with an excited laugh, "Oh, this little one is nice," giving me at the same time a smack on the cheek so violent that her fingers left a mark on the skin. Then she left. At the sight of my crimson cheek the nurse understood at once what had occurred. "Oh, that's nothing," she said, "Miss Z smacks all the new arrivals. Otherwise she's not bad." Despite her words, whenever I saw Miss Z I trembled lest she strike me again.

But what terrified me most was something that took place a few days later. A female patient who had just been hospitalized for having shot another woman in a hotel, came over to my bed crying, "This little girl is a darling," and tickling me, she tried to lift my nightgown and to kiss me, until the nurse came to my relief and scolded her roundly for her perverse behavior. An awful fear and a loathing of her advances petrified me.

Such experiences only added to my agitation and kept me constantly on edge in an attitude of desperate defense, defense against outside perils, defense against inner perils, steeled for the ever-present dangers that threatened me.

I continued to talk a great deal, to give away the packages I received and to write at length to everyone I knew. The avid correspondence, like the knitting, was part of my protective system. I should have written to anyone, talked about anything, so long as I could not hear the plaint of the little inner voice nor concern myself with the System, in which case the doctors would let me out of this hell.

This extraverted behavior probably led to misconceptions on their part. They all thought I was free of the System since I no longer mentioned it. Furthermore, they believed I was asking my friends for packages. How little they knew me! I who was so proud, I who was incapable of asking for the least thing of any sort even from my friends! But appearances were against me. To begin with, I don't know why, all my friends sent me something—candy, fruit, and the like, possibly because it was the holiday season. In any case, I received more packages than ever before in my life. Then I had written to everyone, "Here it is terribly cold; I can't seem to get warm. Something must be missing for me to be so cold."

In writing this, I was referring to my inner cold, to my desolation and to the impossibility of pulling myself together. But never, absolutely never, did I think of physical cold. My friends, however, interpreted what I said in a matter-of-fact way and to my complete amazement several of the closest ones sent me woolens. I could not understand why they sent me things I did not use for I detested woolens and never wore them even in the severest winter weather.

But since I was poor, the doctors figured I was trying to exploit my acquaintances. Actually I kept writing simply to keep myself busy—anything rather than listen to the little voice.

Believing I was deceiving Mama, the doctors set a trap for me. Naturally the letters I wrote to Mama were very different from the others, making no reference to the persons with whom I corresponded nor to the packages I received from them. These things didn't interest me at all. In my despair and suffering, what difference did such things as people or letters or packages make, especially the last, given away as soon as they came? To Mama I had important matters to impart. I did not write her to protect me from the voice but because I wanted to talk to her to tell her all about myself.

This made the doctors suspect that I was hiding from Mama the benefits I enjoyed from others. And one of them suggested that I send all my letters to Mama for stamping! I refused vehemently, considering it an imposition to ask Mama to stamp my letters. I should not have dared to ask her to do this.

At my refusal, the doctors concluded I was a pretty sly one and a profiteer to boot. If the doctors had said simply, "We want you to show your letters to Mrs. Sechehaye," I should not have hesitated; I had nothing to hide from Mama. The whole thing was ridiculous. But by setting this stamp trap they revealed very clearly that they thought me cunning and deceitful.

The tragedy occurred! When Mama came to see me, the doctor told her of the fraud and what he called the "double play" in my eating. For, to go back a little, I had been transferred to a pretty room of my own in the private hospital, and, except for leaving the building, I was completely at liberty. I was, however, eating little; the System's orders forebade me to eat. Since I received many packages (which I turned over to the nurse for the asylum patients) the doctor thought I was stuffing myself with candy and therefore only seemed not to be hungry at meals.

Save for a single fig which I tried to eat despite the System, I did not touch a single package. Nor could I truly say I wasn't hungry; on the contrary I was starved, but the System would not allow me to satisfy the hunger. But I didn't speak of it, because they would have sent me back to the closed ward, which with all my might I did not want.

The doctor recounted all these so-called ruses to Mama when she came to see me. Unfortunately, appearances were against me and she believed him; nor could she conceive that the doctor could be so painfully mistaken. The moment she came to me from his office I knew that something had changed in her attitude to me. But since I was in complete ignorance of the doctor's opinion and what had transpired, I did not know what to make of her coldness.

Again the mad anguish seized me; my little island of reality, my sole refuge was taken from me. At that moment I was convinced that the fault lay in the System, disguising Mama, setting her against me, in order to punish me. This was no less than a sign that it wished my death. For without Mama I could not live. If previously I had doubted the authenticity of the System, this sudden change of Mama's attitude confirmed my belief in it. What had happened was so awful that only the System could have contrived it.

It goes without saying that I fell at once into an unreality more ice-bound and infinite than ever before. Mama left, leaving me with a sense of boundless abandonment and crushing sorrow. I wrote to her immediately, imploring her to tell me what evil I had done or rather what the System had made me do that she no longer loved me. Her answer, guarded and impersonal, only increased my confusion.

The entire defense structure building up since my arrival at the psychiatric hospital gave way and I cried all day and all night. To have lost my only haven, my only help was unbearable. And then I loved Mama so much and here the System had robbed me of her love and her regard. I cogitated on some means of getting rid of myself to escape the System and the horror of my life. Giving my thoughts no truce, I asked myself what wicked thing I had done at the System's instigation, what so wicked as to have lost Mama's love. Indeed, I knew not wherein lay my sin, but the ignorance did not prevent a profound feeling of guilt since Mama appeared angry with me.

That all this stemmed from the doctors' erroneous impressions was far from my thoughts. As an instance, one of them had asked me how I liked the hangings in my room. "Awful," I said. In saying this, I didn't have the least intention of being disagreeable. But at that time, according to my concept of the world, things didn't exist in and of themselves, but each one created a world after his own fashion. Therefore it seemed natural that the doctor should find the hangings pretty, the nurse find them interesting, and I find them awful. The question of social relationships did not touch my spirit in the slightest degree. I have no doubt that I outraged the director's executive pride and that he considered me demanding and badly brought up. The aesthetics of the hangings was a completely abstract matter and left me profoundly indifferent. On such things was my unsavory reputation built.

Three days later, Mama discovered the doctor's mistake and wrote me again as she had formerly. My relief on the receipt of her letter is impossible to describe. I was reborn. Just the same, in spite of my joy, I remained weighed down by a sense of fatality, or rather by the System. For, from that day on, the System was ensconced in my innermost being and I was altogether in its power. At one stroke, it had become stronger than Mama, having succeeded in deceiving her about me, me whom she knew in every respect, who had opened to her the most secret portals of my heart and soul. And in addition, though I feared to return to the disturbed ward, I could no longer pretend about the System and I talked about it to the doctor in spite of myself, so much a part of me was it.

The doctor, assuming I had forgotten about the System, was amazed to discover how alive it was; however, the discovery did not have the expected unpleasant consequences for I soon left that hospital.

I Sink into Unreality

8 For three weeks, Mama made me welcome at her home, which prompted the private hospital in Geneva to take me back. From there I went to my own home, only to fall into a state of apathy. I no longer received orders from the System; there was much less anxiety, and the Fear too affected me rarely. My usually keen sense of responsibility was gone; I did not raise a finger to find work or to help my family. For the greater part of the day I sat in a chair, gazing fixedly before me, or plunged in the absorbed contemplation of a tiny spot; a spot which, no bigger than a grain of pepper, could hold me for an hour without any urge to shift my eyes from their absorption in this microscopic world.

Only a strong force could pull me from it and I dragged myself away to get ready to go to Mama. But with what weariness! The slightest movement required extraordinary effort, particularly to overcome the first inertia. Once I had begun things became easier, but then I could not stop. By extreme exertion of the will I managed to do a little housework or to make dinner. Most of the time, however, I remained sitting uncomfortably, my gaze lost in a drop of coffee fallen on the table.

The fire had gone out and I was cold. I heard the clock strike ten, eleven, half-past eleven and I reflected that it was time to make lunch. With difficulty I shifted my eyes from the drop of coffee to the black stove. But the drop, like a magnet, drew my eyes slowly and persistently to itself. I obeyed and with deep relief plunged again into the limitless world that was the drop of coffee.

From time to time, phrases wandered through my dreaming spirit: "But you will see," or "Perfectly," or even meaningless scraps of words. "Ichtiou, gao, gao!" Finally with a surge of willpower I would get up abruptly and begin to work. But how my eyes struggled! As soon as my gaze fell on a spot of any sort, a shadow or a ray of light, I could not drag it away, caught and held fast by the boundless world of the infinitely small.

To wrench myself out of this impasse I began to beat on the table or on the wall with both fists. But the efficacy of this activity soon exhausted itself. Instead of saving me from the absorbed perception of the spot, in turn I became lost in the automaticity of this substitute behavior. One of my sisters in response to the noise rushed over to stop what she called "this silly game." Nonetheless her intervention helped and enabled me to resume my work. And as the two o'clock appointment for my analytic session approached, I could feel life well up a little in me and my movements grow at once more flexible and energetic.

During the sessions I complained to Mama of the "water that was rising, rising higher, ready to engulf me." To me the water was the torpor that I was managing less and less to overcome. Yet the contact with Mama renewed life and when I returned home I was much more relaxed and less automatic than in the morning.

Sometimes something urged me to sing, to shout at the top of my voice; or I made elaborate plans; to manufacture, for example, a super-comfortable baby carriage in which the infant could travel without inconvenience; or I imagined that everybody had died except me and that I was the earth's only inhabitant with everything at my disposal. Because I no longer struggled against it, I suffered less from unreality itself. Living in an environment empty, artificial and apathetic, an invisible, insuperable wall divided me from people and things. I saw few people and wanted only to be alone, hiding in the cellar where, sitting on the coal pile, I remained quiet, unmoving, my gaze fixed on a spot or a gleam of light.

But behind this wall of indifference, suddenly a wave of anxiety would creep over me, the anxiety of unreality. My perception of the world seemed to sharpen the sense of the strangeness of things. In the silence and immensity, each object was cut off by a knife, detached in the emptiness, in the boundlessness, spaced off from other things. Without any relationship with the environment, just by being itself, it began to come to life. It was there, facing me, terrifying me. And I said, "The chair is making fun of me, it is playing tricks on me."

This was not quite exact, but I did not command the words to express the fear and this keen awareness that the chair was alive and had no other significance.

Sometimes the crises of unreality supervened on the street. Everything looked dead, lifeless, stony, ridiculous, and in the stillness a baby's cry would arouse me and reawaken the fear. I was rejected by the world, on the outside of life, a spectator of a chaotic film unrolling ceaselessly before my eyes, in which I would never have a part. In these awful moments, without protection, inexplicably ill, I could about submit.

In the midst of this agonizing lethargy, storms of dreadful anger, of bitter vexation surged up within me. As a matter of fact, my brothers and sisters annoyed me sorely, especially one sister who was in the habit of taking my nice things and teasing me when I tried to get them back, taunting me with, "Try to get your gloves. Come find them if you want to." This would send me into a frenzied rage and the moment she left the house I would rush to take something of hers and hide it so she could not use it. At once, however, remorse seized me and I was anxious to show that I was not like her, but superior to her. So I took the thing out of hiding and put it back in its place. Our mother always sided with her and scolded me roundly, repeating over and over that I was the eldest and must give way; anyway, sisters always quarreled with each other and pilfered each other's things. These injustices made me miserable and I was relieved to tell everything to Mama who protected and defended me.

These rows with my sister, though innocent in appearance, were all too soul-searing in effect. I hated this sister of whom I was jealous, jealous of her courage, of the easy way she enjoyed life, of her independence, while I was timid, not daring to disobey even when I was within my rights, hesitant to enjoy any kind of pleasure lest I suffer pangs thinking of those less fortunate.

At that time, one of my occupations was walking in front of a psychiatric hospital some distance away, whose manic ward, oddly enough, faced on the street. Indeed, even on entering this street, the screaming and crying were clearly audible. For two hours at a time I could hear a man talking and shouting, and though I did not catch the words I thought I heard him say, "Brothers, brothers, there is immeasurable injustice. Brothers, do not allow it to continue in the world. A dreadful misfortune awaits you. Brothers, I am in intolerable agony. Help, brothers, do not abandon me. I am bowed beneath the weight of excruciating guilt. I am accused of endless crime and I suffer. My situation is inextricable; I am accused on every side; I am innocent but guilty just the same. My suffering is boundless. Can you not help me? Brothers, I am tortured, I am afraid, I am an innocent criminal."

And in his maddened cries, in his imploring sobs, I experienced my own suffering. What never-ending pity I felt for him, how I wanted to help him. And with it mounted the terror that soon I too should come to join him in the "Land of Enlightenment."

After a Beneficial Trip an Acute
Crisis Confounds Me

9 In this state of general lethargy, punctuated by crises of anxiety and hostility towards my brothers and sisters, Mama took me to the seashore for three weeks. This gave me great satisfaction, first because I could be uninterruptedly with Mama, and then I could watch the sea which had always attracted me, yet also inspired some fear.

But I was amazed to discover that the longed-for constant nearness to Mama did not bring the happiness I had anticipated. Quite the contrary; I was disappointed. Before, during our sessions together, Mama had been just "Mama"; now on the trip and at the hotel she became "Mrs. Sechehaye," so that in spite of my wanting it and her kindness and affection, I had no contact with her. She was disguised as a "lady" and in vain I looked for "Mama." Fortunately we had a treatment session every day and I was able to regain the relation, but apart from the sessions she was a stranger. And all my attempts to alter this painful situation were fruitless.

During this holiday, I noticed a complete loss of the sense of perspective. I sketched like a child. I got lost easily and I could not orient myself spatially. The most careful explanations left me without understanding of the cardinal points of direction. To remedy this I placed an imaginary map before me and said to myself: opposite me is the north, behind me is the south, right is east and left is west. But if I suddenly turned around from the areas I had just located and wanted to place what I was facing, I said exactly the same thing as before: opposite me is the north, behind me the south, etc. Neither the sun nor any landmark concerned me at all. I placed the cardinal directions entirely in reference to myself, according to the method I had learned at school, and I was the center: at the top of the map is the north, on the bottom the south, at the right the east, at the left the west. That there was a difference between an unchanging map and changing reality never occurred to me for a moment.

Even the sea disappointed me a little by its artificiality. Nevertheless the change did me good and I dared to disobey the System and eat a great deal more than usual. For a fortnight everything went exceedingly well. But during the last week, the acute attacks of unreality began again when everything appeared vast, detached, brightly lighted. Mama's disguise weighed on me; I suffered miserably because, unable to recognize her at all except for the one hour each day, I had lost contact with her.

Then, basically, I was vexed with her for allowing the System to effect the disguise. Why wasn't she stronger? Why did "Mama" hide all the time save for a brief period? Nor did I dare to tell her I was annoyed, not because I wanted to cover up my annoyance, but I knew she was under the System's influence and would never dare attack the System by criticizing its activities.

In the sessions my whole energy was strained toward finding Mama again and when finally contact with her was established, I drank deep at the spring to give me support for the rest of the day. I never dreamed of announcing my vexation. And what would complaining have accomplished? Mama would not understand; she would only answer that she had not ceased to be herself and that I was laboring under a misapprehension. As for me, I was convinced that, without knowing it, she was a toy in the hands of the System and I was wretched over her transformation.

Then, too, the social effort I had to make at the hotel further increased the feeling of unreality. Added to this, the fact that I ate as I liked, in defiance of the System's prohibitions, markedly augmented the guilt in the face of this disobedience; the more so since a considerable gain in weight took on the aspects of an extra impurity.

Toward the end of our stay, the System became more insistent. Feeling guilty, I was driven to run from the hotel and hide among the rocks near the shore. Knowing me so well, Mama easily guessed where I was and understood that the caves beside the sea formed a perfect refuge where I might hide and find shelter. The orders grew more pressing: I was to throw myself into the sea; I was to open a vein. But more urgently, I was to find my way to the water's bottom. It was this that drove me to hide in a gloomy little cavern to escape the System's persecution.

On the eve of our departure I could not sleep. I felt compelled to rise, to flee, to do myself harm. I no longer cared about the people at the hotel, about the conventions, as though at one stroke I had dropped the social ties weighing so heavily. Mama administered sedatives, and half-asleep, I returned to Geneva. Mama took me to the hospital where the doctor put me to bed at once.

The state of indifference reigning until now was abruptly replaced by inner and outer agitation. At first I felt obliged to get up and walk; it was impossible to stay in bed. Singing a requiem without pause, I marched three steps forward and three steps back, an automatism that wearied me exceedingly and which I wished some one would help me break. I could not do it alone, for I felt forced to make these steps and if I stopped from exhaustion, even for a moment, I felt guilty again. Moreover, when any behavior became automatic, I felt guilty in interrupting it. But no one could believe that I wanted to stop, for as soon as they made me give up some stereotyped procedure, I began anew.

People appeared as in a dream. I no longer distinguished their individual personalities. They were "human beings"; that was all. In each one I saw mankind and in consequence I addressed them all familiarly. If I were lost in a great desert and met someone, would I care about his name, about his individual personality? It was enough that he was a member of the race. And so I took to saying as though we were old friends, "Good-day, nurse, how goes it?" or "Doctor, what do you say to my getting out of bed?" using the intimate form of address.

At the beginning of my stay, everything seemed funny, old, ridiculous. In my mania, even the System seemed peculiar and I began to call its head "Antipiol," the name of a salve used on sores in the hospital. I localized him on my right, and when I spoke to him I always turned in that direction. But I neither saw nor heard him. Nevertheless, I answered him and I was annoyed at what he said, crying, "No, no, I don't want to, Antipiol, keep quiet, I won't listen to you any more, no, no, no!" My anger was sincere and spontaneous; still, I answered to emptiness, yet not emptiness, not real silence. Sometimes I stopped up my ears in dread, especially the right ear, I was so exasperated. But exasperated with what?

I threw things to the right, toward the locked French windows where I localized my Persecutor, the System, Antipiol—pillows, the water pitcher, my comb. I wanted to chase Antipiol, to crush him so that I would no longer hear his voice.

Actually, in all honesty, I saw no one. I heard no voice. Yet there it was, not an emptiness, not a silence. There was a considerable difference between this part of the room and the others. The corner at the right was alive, personalized; there was someone very real there, empty though it was.

Indeed, before me battalions of personages in greatcoats passed and repassed ominously and interminably. Trying to catch them I encountered nothing, my hand fell into space. Shouts, howls and deafening noises roared in my head, but here again my ear actually heard nothing. Forced to cry out these senseless things I repeated "Battle of Trafalgar—Destruction by fire—absolute—absolute—gao, gao."

Some time later as the comical aspect of things disappear, the surrounding world grew dreamlike. The orders, or rather impulses, persuaded me to harm myself. I bit my hands, my arms, cruelly; I beat my head against the wall; I struck my chest so hard with my fist I was covered with bruises and it was necessary to protect me from myself. An inconceivable urge to destruction rose in me, an urge to annihilate myself at all costs. And I was profoundly guilty, a guilt vast and horrible, unbearable, remorseless; of what I knew not, yet deeply, immeasurably guilty. I would not eat; by any means I tried to destroy myself. Only Mama was able to prevent it.

When she showed me something white, such as my sheet, saying, "You see, this lovely whiteness means that you are not guilty; this is proof of it," I was much relieved. But unfortunately my agitated condition didn't allow me to listen long even to Mama. Too much noise, too much movement, too many thoughts disputed within me, and furthermore, I had lost real contact with Mama. I always watched her come with joy, but she seemed unreal, artificial.

This state lasted several months. I was transferred to a private psychiatric hospital where I was kept in a constant bath. I continued to respond to voices which, though I actually did not hear them, existed nonetheless for me. From this instititute I went to another where I became more tranquil. I spoke to no one, yet I was quite aware of everything that went on about me. Except for moments of agitation or intense crises of guilt, I fell again into complete apathy. The world was a moving picture, taking place without my participation. When they insisted I answer questions, I made a great effort to try to cooperate. But if I succeeded in bringing forth some phrases, the effort, the struggle, caused intense excitement and reawakened a hostility to people, and incoherent, groundless aggressiveness, and immediately afterward extreme guilt overcame me and I cried and wept for hours. Little by little I fell back into unreality where everything was detached, electrical, metallic.

My First Double:
The Little Monkey

10 Some time later, Mama, whom I saw rarely, took me to Geneva and placed me in the home of a nurse; here she came to see me every day.

However, for three weeks she was away on a trip and I was left to myself in this unfamiliar house. I ate practically nothing, for everything was forbidden. The System forbade anything salted or sweetened. I drank a great deal of tea and ate spinach since it was green and a product of the soil.

After I left the hospital I no longer heard Antipiol's voice. I say "heard" for I do not know what other word to use to convey the impression of actually hearing an invisible something occupying a corner of the room and saying disagreeable things to which I was obliged to answer. Just the same, I did not really hear them. At this time, nothing of this sort bothered me. Instead there was the desert, the cold within me, the vastness without limit, a country of infinite desolation and despair.

I passed the days in a chair, my eyes bent on a spot, or I rested in the orchard under the bright sun, held motionless by a blade of grass or a ray of light. Sometimes I walked in the country, straight ahead, nearly running, finding it always difficult to come back again.

Finally Mama returned and I saw her nearly every day. I was happy at her return for I felt abandoned and also because I was again experiencing the impulse to harm myself, to hit my head against the wall, to bite and mutilate myself.

Mama brought me a gift—a little plush monkey of which I was at once afraid. When he had his arms up, I was anxious lest he hurt me; and then, he had a most shockingly unhappy expression. Oddly, at that very moment, I felt the impulse to strike myself. I realized full well that my own arms were delivering the blows, still I was sure the monkey was attacking me. Nonetheless I did not know that he was a symbol of myself, nor in any case should I have known what that meant.

I said to myself, "I am I and he is he and there is no relationship between us;" however the confusion as to who was who was complete. He had the same troubles as I and moreover he wanted to hurt me, to destroy me, and I dreaded him without holding it against him for I realized it was not his fault.

When I related my fears to Mama she did something extraordinary: She took the monkey's two arms, lowered them around his little knees and said, "Mama's little monkey, Mama asks you always to keep your arms down to comfort Renee. Then Renee will not be afraid of you, do you see?" The little monkey agreed; I could see it in his eyes. It is hard to express how relieved I was that Mama made him take this position. At any rate, from that moment, the impulse to self harm left me abruptly.

I was very careful to see that the monkey kept his arms down. Were they perchance up I was forced to stike myself since the monkey wished it. Then I would run to him and lower his arms. And everything was well again.

The Miracle of the Apples

11 The monkey was very unhappy because he had nothing to eat; everything was forbidden him except apples and spinach. So I went to the orchard to gather an apple or two from the tree; these I ate voraciously. In taking these apples, I had no sense of guilt for the tree was part of my country, the land of Tibet I called it, of which I was queen. Indeed, I had the clear impression of living in a desert country, desolate, rocky, unreal, where I had one right—to eat the apples of my tree. Nevertheless, despite the tree, I was abandoned, miserable, left only the right to eat the apples; everything else was denied me.

Mama brought me pounds of magnificent apples. But I could not touch them, for I was allowed to eat only my own apples still attached to their Mama-tree. I should have liked so much to have Mama give me apples, real apples I called them.

But, alas, Mama did not understand. Amazed, she cried, "But aren't all these apples that I bring you real? Why don't you eat them?" Her words irritated me and I removed myself more and more from Mama. I had no more contact with her except when she took the little monkey in her arms and talked to him, a thing she did too rarely to suit me.

I was extremely unhappy. I felt myself getting younger; the System wanted to reduce me to nothing. Even as I diminished in body and in age, I discovered that I was nine centuries old. For to be nine centuries old actually meant being not yet born. That is why the nine centuries did not make me feel at all old; quite the contrary.

More and more a criminal guilt weighed me down. Now my punishment consisted in the transformation of my hands into cat's paws. I had a dreadful fear of my hands and the conviction that I would be changed into a famished cat, prowling in cemeteries, forced to devour the remains of decomposing cadavers. Added to this, I was again being watched, attacked and jeered at by the head of the System, Antipiol. He took up his position at the further end near the closet on the right. Mocking voices sneered at me: "Ah, ah, wretched creature, eat, eat, only eat, do eat!" They kept urging me to eat, knowing it was forbidden and that I would be severely punished if I acceded to their prompting.

At these times my ear took some part in hearing the voices. This was not so before when I responded to the voices without any auditory sensation. Now even though I distinguished them readily from real voices, I could say I actually heard them resounding in my room. And then I kept seeing everything in a confusion of terrible unreality, each object cut off, under a cold and blinding light.

More and more I lost contact with Mama, and it often happened that I avoided her and even forgot her visit, something practically unheard of for me. For Mama remained the sole being to whom I still clung in my despair.

One day I directed my steps toward my apple tree and plucked a green apple. I was about to carry it to my lips when the farmer's wife who owned this part of the land came up to me and said, "Ah, hah! I've been watching you for a long time; it's not the first time I've seen you taking the apples from my trees. You're going to stop this business right away or else . . ." Without waiting for her to continue I dropped the apple and fled to my room, locked the door and barricaded it with furniture.

The horror that gripped me on hearing these words is impossible to describe. Shame, rage, the deceit, and above all an intolerable burden of blame struggled in my heart. Prostrated on the floor, in the darkest corner of my room, I wept and cried out in anguish. The most appalling misfortune seemed to have befallen me. Completely abandoned, stripped, I was persuaded that a will, an irresistible authority, wished me dead. The one favor, my only remaining sanction, had just been brutally wrenched away and my awful guilt put in its place.

Desolate, I continued to cry: "Give me my apples, give me my apples, Renee is hungry, give me my apples, Renee is hungry." An indescribable wrath mounted against the wicked farm-wife who had taken from me my right to sustenance, my right to live. But she had done it, had robbed me; she must then be right and I wrong to want the apples. The more I wanted them, the more I demanded "my apples" back again, the heavier lay the load of guilt. I wept and cried for hours, trembling when anyone knocked on the door and called, certain that the police were coming for me to put me to death. In the far corner of the room, the voices, derisive and harsh, tormented me with taunts and threats. By an unhappy coincidence, my little monkey raised his arms with a menacing gesture. He too wanted to kill me.

At length the nurse succeeded in getting into the room by opening the door, locked on the inside, through a grating opening on the outside. She administered a sedative, put me to bed and I fell asleep.

The next morning all the horror of the previous day seized me anew. Rising, I dressed hurriedly and fled the hospital, running straight ahead. I walked for several hours, crossed the frontier, and began to climb a mountain path. It was autumn and a heavy fog hung around. On the narrow road a benign indifference spread over me.

Climbing higher and higher, at length I reached the top about a thousand meters up. There, spent with fatigue, with hunger and exhaustion, I rested for awhile. My head was empty; I thought of nothing, obedient only to an impulse pushing me ever onward. A woman appeared suddenly, questioned me, wanted to know where I came from, where I was going, and if I wanted to have something at the inn. She could hardly believe I had actually come all the way from Geneva. Since she was insistent, I had to tell her I had no money and could not go to the inn.

Something about me must have astonished her, for she advised me to return home to my Mama. She helped me rise and accompanied me for the next two hours on the way back.

It was now evening. I had been on the road since nine o'clock that morning and I was at the end of my strength. My feet were torn and bleeding and I moved like an automaton. In a state of near-unconsciousness brought on by exhaustion I went up to my room where I found Mama extremely upset. She took charge of me, undressed me, gave me a warm bath and only left me when I fell asleep. I told her the story of the farmer's wife.

The next morning weariness kept me in bed a part of the day. But in the evening, the nurse forced me to go down to dinner instead of bringing me the usual tray. I obeyed her and even ate a little. But the effort I had to make to descend and mingle with the other guests exceeded my strength. A horrible agitation rose in me, hostility mixed with insuperable anxiety and particularly an infinite sense of guilt for having dared to eat. The longing for my apples reached such a peak that I did not know what was to become of me. At that moment I was certain that if I remained longer without apples and if in addition, by forcing me to go to the table, they compelled me to such exacting social behavior, I could not go on living.

In a state of distraction, strangeness and unheard of anguish, at nine o'clock that evening I ran on foot to Mama's house. In my ears the voices sneered, threatened me with death. My hands, like cat's paws, filled me with fear. At the same time I seemed to grow smaller and the nine centuries weighed heavily on my spirit. A tempest of horror, of desolation, of unreality, of hopeless abandonment roared in my soul.

The voices were screaming, crying out that I ought to throw myself in the river. But I resisted with all my strength as I ran to Mama. At last I reached there and threw myself into her arms, weeping and stammering, "They made me eat, they forced me to, and then the farmer's wife scolded me; I have nothing any more, I have no more apples; I'm going to die."

Mama tried affectionately to calm me, but without success. "Why," she said, "don't you take the apples I bring you?" "I can't do that, Mama," I answered. And while in my heart I was outraged that Mama too wanted to force me to eat, my eyes fell to her bosom, and when she insisted, "But why don't you want the apples I buy you?" I knew what I was yearning for so desperately and I was able to bring out, "Because the apples you buy are food for grown-ups and I want real apples. Mama's apples, like those," and I pointed to Mama's breasts.

She got up at once, went to get a magnificent apple, cut a piece and gave it to me, saying, "Now, Mama is going to feed her little Renee. It is time to drink the good milk from Mama's apples." She put the piece in my mouth, and with my eyes closed, my head against her breast, I ate, or rather drank, my milk. A nameless felicity flowed into my heart. It was as though, suddenly, by magic, all my agony, the tempest which had shaken me a moment ago, had given place to a blissful calm; I thought of nothing, I discerned nothing, I reveled in my joy. I was fully content, with a passive contentment, the contentment of a tiny baby, quite unconscious, for I did not even know what caused it.

When I had finished my "meal" of the apple, Mama told me that next morning I could have it again and that she would give orders to the nurse, but she would come herself to give me the piece of apple.

I left with the nurse who had come to fetch me, and when we were outside I realized that my perception of things had completely changed. Instead of infinite space, unreal, where everything was cut off, naked and isolated, I saw Reality, marvelous Reality, for the first time. The people whom we encountered were no longer automatons, phantoms, revolving around, gesticulating without meaning; they were men and women with their own individual characteristics, their own individuality. It was the same with things. They were useful things, having sense, capable of giving pleasure. Here was an automobile to take me to the hospital, cushions I could rest on. With the astonishment that one views a miracle, I devoured with my eyes everything that happened. "This is it, this is it," I kept repeating, and I was actually saying, "This is it—Reality."

As I entered my room after arriving at the hospital, it was no longer my room, but living, sympathetic, real, warm. And to the stupefaction of the nurse, for the first time I dared to handle the chairs, to change the arrangement of the furniture. What unknown joy, to have an influence on things; to do with them what I liked and especially to have the pleasure of wanting the change. Until now I had tolerated no change, even the slightest. Everything had to be in order, regular, symmetrical. That night I slept very well.

A new day dawned. I was happy, but rather awkwardly happy, for I was frail as a chick just out of the egg. The nurse gave me the piece of apple cut by Mama which I "drank," leaning my cheek on a large apple that Mama gave me after holding it against her breast. For me, this apple was sacred, as Mama's bosom had been the day before. Later, she arrived and I ate or rather "drank" my milk-apple lying against her breast in ineffable happiness.

During this second day, I realized that the voices had disappeared and particularly that I no longer risked being changed into a cat. I enjoyed everything I saw, everything I touched. For the first time I was in touch with reality. Mama too had changed in my eyes. Before she had appeared like an image, a statue that one likes to look at, though it remains artificial, unreal; but from this moment on she became alive, warm, animated, and I cherished her deeply. I had an intense desire to remain near her, against her, to preserve this marvelous contact.

But it was only an "oral" contact, that is, it was only as "Mama-nourishment" that I could have intimate contact with her; every other consideration but "my apples" was indifferent and inimical to me.

During the days that followed, I had several alarms, for Mama tried to make me eat like the others, nearly causing me to lose my balance. It was as though my world were to be turned topsy-turvy, to be set awry, and unutterable anxiety permeated my being. Fortunately, Mama understood that I could only move slowly. After the raw apples (breast-milk) I could take apples as apple-sauce, preceded by a quarter of a raw apple, and finally an unpeeled apple.

Progressively, I could eat real milk and porridge, something unheard of, for until that day I detested milk. But at that time it seemed altogether natural to drink milk.

On the mantelpiece were always two beautiful apples representing the maternal breasts given me by Mama to protect me. At the least anxiety I ran to them and at once was reassured. I felt so new, so content that I agreed to make some little things in raffia; I was the more interested because they were intended for Mama.

I Learn to Know My Body

12 Some time later, my interest in maternal nourishment waned and I focused instead on my body. But I dared not concern myself with it lest it cover me with guilt. Quite astonishingly, however, Mama knew that deep within me I wanted to be clean, pretty and neat, but that I had no right.

She brought a lightly scented soap and gave the nurse strict orders to bathe me every day. Mama was present at one or two baths; she said, "Mama wants Renee to be very clean and neat; Mama wants Renee to take a bath so she will be." What a satisfaction to lie in the lovely, warm, fragrant water, as though I lay in Mama's arms. Just the same, the privilege of washing with this soap, of washing at all, was not for me. But I could accept the nurse's washing me because under these conditions I was not responsible for the pleasure I experienced in being clean.

Unhappily, Mama did not comprehend the intense culpability ready to sweep over me the moment I took the initiative in creating the pleasure myself. She said something dreadful: "Bathe Renee only when she wants to; she loves it, don't you, Renee?"

A tearing rage against Mama rose up in me. How could she do anything like that to me, anything so shameful! To declare openly that it was I, Renee, who wanted the pleasure of a bath! The blame attached to this was immediately reawakened and I vehemently refused to bathe.

At once contact between Mama and me was disrupted; abruptly wonderful reality disappeared, to be replaced by the old cinematographic scene. I was crushed by the responsibility she had laid on me and deeply wounded that she had said aloud in front of the nurse that I enjoyed the bath and wanted it. However, by refusing to bathe and remaining quite passive while the nurse washed me, I managed to temper a little my unbearable guilt.

As a consequence of this break of contact, I turned more toward the nurse who took care of me and whom I liked very much. In spite of this, hostile impulses against her would surge up suddenly for no apparent reason.

Mama's Other Patients; All My
Self-Destructive Energies
Are Unleashed

13 Months passed; then one day my nurse failed to appear as usual. She had gone on vacation, causing me a horrible shock. All night long I sobbed in anger and grief; my whole world had fallen to pieces. Her absence was simply unbearable and my suffering was cruel. Then, too, I was vexed with Mama for allowing her to leave. Though at that time I went to spend several weeks at Mama's home, I felt a pervasive sense of abandonment, for it had been the nurse who had fed me, dressed me and made me work a little.

It was early in the nurse's absence when I first began to recognize the fact that Mama had patients and that she had a husband whom I called the "Great Personage." I was left quite to myself, passing the days in a chair, my eyes cast down, waiting until Mama had finished with her patients. I could not bear the thought that she was giving a large part of her time to strangers, leaving me alone with the System and with the newly returned voices. Furthermore, I was now excessively rigid, every movement a source of pain, even to altering the direction of my gaze. Sunk in deep apathy, broken by crises of insensate rage against Mama because of her patients, I dared not openly reveal my hostility. Mama was a powerful queen, a formidable divinity whom one must avoid antagonizing. This Goddess was unfair, giving of her sacredly precious milk to the undeserving whose needs were not as pressing as mine.

From her personal and telephone conversations with them, I realized that the patients coming to Mama enjoyed a freedom in life denied to me. They went on excursions, to parties, to the movies, while I—I struggled alone with the importunate voices or remained immobile, frozen, uncomfortable in a chair.

Mama I recognized less and less; in her place I perceived the Queen, the Goddess, source of life and joy, yet withal a source of deprivation as well. For could she not take back what she had given? I drew up several bills of complaint, or rather of supplication, to point out to her her injustice to the "Little Queen of Tibet" or the "Little Iron Bar" as I called myself.

With each indictment I believed the Queen would understand and bestow the precious milk. But, alas, she did not comprehend my language, the language I used in talking to myself, comprising words discrete and unrelated and others self-created since I was denied the privilege of writing real words. Indeed, in such a case, the Queen would have been justified in punishing me, for the bill of complaints was full of animosity and protest. When I wrote in "the language" it was to the Mama of the "apples," the one who loved me and whom I loved. But the Mama of the apples did not understand; the Queen, formidable and terrible, had completely supplanted her.

During this period, I had been twice admitted to the psychiatric institution where I talked to no one and returned to Mama even more rigid, more silent and particularly more inimical and guilty. The Queen showed displeasure when I tried to admonish Mama.

One day, after tying together all the shoes I could find, I hung them on the key of the wardrobe, and on the key I balanced a pair of open scissors, the sharp points up. By this I intended to apprise Mama of my annoyance and the fact that she was to take care of me as I had orders to leave. The shoes were to signify departure; their disarray, anger; the string the tension of unreality; the scissors represented the aggression as well as the means open to Mama to rout the anger and cut the tension. But it was the Queen who remarked that my composition was dangerous and she took it apart.

Finally one day at dinner, more unhappy and upset about the patients than ordinarily, I refused to eat. Mama, instead of insisting, instead of announcing that she, Mama, gave me the right to eat, exclaimed, "You may leave it, if you don't want to eat it," meaning, to me, "I don't want you to eat!" I rose and ran to my room, weeping and wailing in fathomless despair.

Mama came to comfort me, but I hardly knew her. During the evening an awful rage against myself surged up. I detested, I loathed myself, I deserved death. I sobbed in hate and in guilt and struck myself with violence. I was in a turmoil. Voices screamed at me, "You wretch, you have no right to live; you criminal, you have committed the crime of Cain." The doctor came and administered two effective hypodermics; but the next morning it began again, and my affliction was unalleviated. All the self-destructive forces were reactivated, hurling themselves furiously against me, trying to demolish me. Nothing now could check them, for not only did Mama refuse to feed me as she did the others, but she had forbidden me to eat, showing clearly she did not love me and had rejected me. They took me again to the hospital, kept me in a constant bath, guarded by a nurse who held my arms behind me lest I injure myself. There the deadly self-hate continued to manifest itself. I wanted to die; I ought to have died.

Before my eyes I saw a fat cow coming at me with her horns. This was Mama and my fear was ghastly. On every side voices howled, jeered at me, mocked me, and I screamed in torturing guilt, in animosity and in despondency. I cried out, "See what you have done, you wretches, you robbers, you ghouls feeding on breasts; see, see what you have done?" It was at Mama's other patients, the fountainhead of my misfortunes, that I flung these imprecations.

At length, under the influence of the baths, of sedatives, and of fatigue, I fell into a state of stupor, supine on my bed, motionless in an indifference permeating and absolute. The doctors and nurses concluded I knew no one; but this was not the case. Rather the constricting apathy made for an inner emptiness preventing the display of any sign. When I saw Mama again I recognized her, and while the nurse held my eyes open, I even noticed that she was weeping. I felt some movement in her direction and I wanted to say something, but all that came was, "I, I—home, home—Mama, Mama."

Mama understood my pitiful wish to stay with her and she took me home. When I reached my room, a sense of deliverance swept over me and, though I had been artificially fed up to now, I demanded "Bread, bread, bread," and managed to eat a little.

For nearly a year, partly with Mama, more often at the hospital, I continued sunk in this condition of congealed lethargy, lying with my knees up, my head turned to the wall, my hair covering my face in order to see no one. From time to time an episode of guilt and hopeless despair broke the monotonous succession of days. In my fantasy, entire cities lay in ruins, rocks crushed in fragments, all a consequence of my execrable crime, the sin of Cain.

One day while I was crying forlornly Mama brought me some whipped cream, and placing a spoonful of it in my mouth said, "Take some white snow; it will purify Renee. When Mama gives Renee the snow, the crime will disappear; Renee will be pure again." And with the snow, my penetrating guilt, my sense of unworthiness were at once tempered. I took courage and dared to move a bit. The movement, however, inspired a temerity that brought havoc in its wake.

One of my sisters came to see me and in front of Mama I gave her a little slap and then I raised my arm but without touching her. This upset Mama and she said to my sister, "Go, leave at once before Renee attacks you." To me, Mama's words implied protection for my sister and disapproval of me. Immediately, the old guilt overpowered me and threatening voices accused me of the biblical evil. More guilt I could not carry. Mama again offered me the cream, but this time I declined it vehemently; I was too liable, too unworthy to dare accept it. Mama returned to the charge, and already, in the face of her insistence, the hope of pardon glimmered in my soul. But, alas, at my repeated refusals, she desisted too soon in the proffer of forgiveness. Could she have surmised the cries of supplication beating in my breast, imploring her to force me to the "snow" of remission; had she at that moment placed the cream in my mouth, I would have been spared the horror that followed. Unhappily, she did not suspect my intense, unspoken need to be granted indulgence by the snow. She was only the outer screen, an obstinate resistance, a confused agitation.

When I realized she was forsaking me to

the crime of Cain, my agony knew no bounds. I shrieked with pain under this mortal burden; I could do no other. An inchoate, indefinable blame bore me down beneath a herculean load, liberating all the self-destructive energies within me. I was no longer cognizant of where I was or what I was doing. Only one thing absorbed me, to annihilate, to assassinate this ignoble being, this hideous, infamous creature, myself, hated to the point of death. The voices were unchained afresh; a devastating tempest ravaged my soul.

Then again back to the mental hospital where shortly I fell into a state of all-embracing stupor and indifference. Everything passed as in a dreary dream; nothing was differentiated, no reaction was possible. Neither the doctors nor the nurses assumed any comprehension of their orders and questions. Yet they were mistaken; I was perfectly aware of what went on, of what was said about me. Indeed, everything had become so totally irrelevant, so devoid of emotion and sensibility that in truth it was the same as though they were not talking to me at all. I simply could not react, the essential motor force had broken down. Images with whom I had nothing to do, from whom I was remote, moved toward and away from my bed. I was, myself, a lifeless image.

When I saw Mama again, something re-awoke in me and I made a prodigious effort to establish warm contact with her. Despite this exertion of my will I could only stammer. "I, I, me, I, me," that was all.

In this eerie atmosphere of torpor and mutism the months passed, marked only by the wracking crises of guilt and antagonism. The voices attacked me, threatened me, demanded my death. Then Mama gave me a beautiful plush tiger and, taking it from her, I recognized him as my defender which alone, with Mama, could shield me from harm. The relief was tremendous for when I wanted to revenge myself against the evil-doers, it was he who took my place, loving me and biting those who would do me injury. The distinction he made between them and me made me proud; I was his chosen one and he was ready to leap against those who wished me ill. He was "Mama" who pro-tected me and preferred me to the other patients.

The periods of confounding guilt persisted along with bitter moral pain and I shed tears for hours, crying, "Raïte, Raïte, was habe ich gemacht?" (What have I done?), sorrowing in my own "language", in the meaningless, recurring syllables, "icthiou, gao, itivare, giastow, ovede" and the like. In no way did I seek to create them; they came of themselves and by themselves meant nothing. Only the sound, the rhythm of the pronunciation had sense. Through them I lamented, pouring out the grueling grief and the interminable sadness in my heart. I could not use ordinary words, for my pain and sorrow had no real basis.

The System, the Country of Tibet, even the voices had lost their emotional power and ceased to interest me. The voices said silly things, but were otherwise innocuous. Sunk beyond language, beyond thought, I reflected no more on the murder of Abel. Only the aridity of the desert remained, broken by patches of searing moral pain, the sound of splintering rock cracking under ponderous destructive force. At these times I was transformed into a fury of self-annihilation, bent by any means on making an end. Nor was this violence now linked to ideas or to orders, but a violence existing of itself, a guilt and pain unalloyed, and by this token the more intense and intolerable than when accompanied by thoughts.

Exhausted by these crises lasting for days, I would fall into the dull inertia, still pursued by the impulses to self-destruction, impulses lacking any element of feeling or emotion.

Mama is Busy with Baby Ezekiel

14 I was present when Mama first held a doll in her arms, a baby doll whom I named Ezekiel. She covered him, kissed him affectionately, put him to bed in his cradle. In the beginning it was enough for me to watch him avidly. All at once I experienced profound amazement that Ezekiel should receive Mama's love and affection without the occurrence of anything untoward. At any moment I expected Mama to cast Ezekiel off because *I* did not deserve to live. In my mind reigned utter confusion concerning Ezekiel and me. When Mama held him in her arms, I trembled lest she drop him precipitously in his cradle, and if she did, I had the uncanny impression that it was I who had been so treated.

Taking courage one day when Ezekiel was in Mama's arms, I pushed his head forward on her bosom to test whether I had the right to live. At this, Mama pressed him to her breast and let him nurse. This she did regularly several times a day so that I awaited the moment in fear of her forgetting. But Mama did not forget and I began to dare to live.

The self-destructive impulses decreased perceptibly, and instead of spending the day in bed with my head under the covers, I looked about me, interested in everything concerning Ezekiel. Then I, who had always refused food, even presumed to eat. A little later when I saw how Mama bathed and dressed Ezekiel, I consented with pleasure to being bathed and dressed myself and actually enjoyed it. In busying herself lovingly with Ezekiel it was as though Mama were bestowing on me the right to live. Slowly I came out of the lethargy and grew more and more interested in what Mama said and did to Ezekiel, an interest confined strictly, however, to feeding and cleanliness. I allowed myself to enjoy it a bit; even so, the dreadful crises of guilt persisted.

I Enter Mama's Body and Am Reborn in Ezekiel

15 A severe attack of pyelonephritis accompanied by agonizing renal pain contrived to stimulate the crises markedly. Far from appeasing the guilt, the pain served to augment it, and since I suffered excruciatingly I recognized this as a sure and terrible sign of blameworthiness. Just when I had the greatest need of Mama she fell gravely ill and for several weeks I was in the care of a nurse.

Naturally I did not understand that Mama's illness prevented her taking care of me; I considered her omnipotent and if she did not appear to tend Ezekiel it was proof that she had abandoned me, that I was not to go on living. At once, the self-destructive impetus and the waiting voices awoke again with fresh energy. I cowered in body and soul and my single yearning was to regain the paradise of Mama's body, a paradise guilty and forbidden since she did not accept me.

Finally the physical malady abated, yet the impulses and the voices stayed on. One day when Mama was well and I was tortured by their persecution, she came to me and announced her intention of banishing the voices, thereby enabling me to sleep like Ezekiel and Moses. After a sedative hypodermic injection, I shortly felt myself slipping into a wonderful realm of peace. Everything in the room was green, green as the sea, quite like being in Mama's body. My pain assuaged in a state of perfect passivity, without want of any kind; Mama had procured this bliss for me. Hence, I thought, she is willing to take me into her body. An immense relief flowed over me; I was in Paradise, in the maternal bosom.

From that moment I had unshakable confidence in Mama and I loved her as never before. That she had received me into herself, that she had acceded to my fondest wish filled me with happiness and proved without doubt that she loved me, that I was loved. Whenever after this the suffering bore me down and the voices afflicted me, by the simple expedient of a sedative hypodermic and arranging the green twilight in my room, Mama placed me in the "green sea," in felicity, safe from every vicissitude.

But when there was no suffering, my greatest joy was to lie peacefully in the green light, my hand in Mama's, Ezekiel on her heart. My contact with Mama persisted without interruption. Her sweet voice alone sufficed now to soothe the voices and the impulses. And more and more, I preferred to be *near* her, rather than *within* her. I feared nothing since she could let me enter the twilight when I wished.

Mama had resumed her care of Ezekiel. And I, I became more courageous in my conviction of Mama's love; for had she not given me the ultimate proof? As Ezekiel took nourishment from her, so did I and I was even anxious to feed myself. This was a tremendous urge to independence, but hardly had it been formulated when the anxiety of being cast away seized me anew.

However, Mama refused to let me eat alone, certain evidence that she did not mean to forsake me, that she wanted to nourish me. My belief in her love was strengthened and soon I actually dared to feed myself if she were close to me.

Later Mama gave me a letter in which was noted in detail what food I was to eat, food she herself had prepared, so that even in her absence she was near me. And I talked of her to myself which helped a great deal. The growing independence in eating was a long step toward reality.

Since Mama had received me in the "sea" (in her body) my perception of reality had quite changed. She was again as she had been after the "apples," vibrant, animated, warm. Only my interest was limited, circumscribed by those things I had shared with Mama or that had passed through her hands. Nonetheless what I saw was beautiful reality. Mama to me was a miraculous cow, not in any way like the ordinary cow, the simple animal one sees in pastures or in pictures, but something altogether different, a divine being before whom I was ready to genuflect in adoration. This indeed I did before a wall whereon I saw delineated the outlines of my cow.

For all my interests I looked to Mama. When I saw her dress Ezekiel, I was emboldened to find interest in my own body, the more that Mama admired it. Nothing made me prouder and happier than to hear Mama say, "What a nice body little Renee has, how clean it is," and I was encouraged to care for and to love my own body.

Of the greatest importance and a primary contribution to growing self-awareness and freedom from guilt in self-esteem, was

Mama's manner of speaking to me. I could never accept her addressing me in the second person, "*You* have a nice body, how clean *you* are." This would have aroused devastating anxiety and anger against Mama for laying such a sin on me. To say, "*You, your* body," would be to place the responsibility on me; while by personifying my body, "It is nice, this body that is going to be washed and scented," was to separate me from it. It became something independent of me, resembling Ezekiel. Mama washed it, found it nice; and little by little, like Mama I could wash it; I could do it since I was imitating Mama. Finally, when for some time I had done it with Mama, I was able to do it without her so long as I talked to it exactly as she did, to take the responsibility, to like it. Then I permitted myself to say, "*My* body, *I* am washing it, *I* am pretty." Through Mama I had learned to like myself, to achieve the integrity of my ego.

If, however, I attempted something unrelated to Mama, I at once lost interest and the drive toward self-destruction was reactivated. Concomitantly the outlook on reality was abruptly transmuted. The warm, living, real surroundings expanded weirdly, objects drew apart in isolation, separated from one another. A country, mineral, limitless, cosmically desolate, stretched around me. And a wall of ice cut me off from people.

As I moved progressively toward reality, these states became more infrequent, depending exclusively on my emotional relation with Mama. At first I could maintain contact with Mama only if she met me on the level at which I was. Any other kind of conversation or social attitude on her part removed me from reality and I could accept her only as part of the outside world. Then by degrees I became independent of her, first through feeding, then through cleanliness and personal care. At length I could think differently from her without endangering clear reality perception.

I Become Firmly Established
in Wonderful Reality

16 Soon I observed that I loved Mama for herself and not in relation to my need to possess all of her. Increasingly greater segments of her social personality were incorporated in my love. And when we were walking, or in a trolley, or at the moving pictures, I knew her full well, whereas formerly I had found her disguised, unrecognizable, the moment she assumed a social attitude toward me, no matter how affectionate, or broke our contact by the use of language other than my own.

Progressively reality was reconstituted and I became more peaceful and free. I was particularly relaxed amidst nature, in the woods, at the seashore, far from the stares of people. Subsequently I began to enjoy city pleasures, the large stores, the vivacity, the tearooms.

One rugged barrier had still to be cleared—the matter of the patients. Before Mama sided with me and cared for me through Ezekiel, I endured pangs of envy. When patients stayed more than an hour, I was consumed with jealousy, resentment and fear, even though I was sure of Mama's love. But at such times I was carried away by a tempest and could think of nothing else. I sat tense against the radiator, looking out the window, and, as so many times before, everything would suddenly grow unreal, hallucinatory, transformed. When finally Mama came to lance this "abscess" of the patients, as I called it, at once beautiful and living reality reappeared and I felt an invigorated contact with her.

Having at last hurdled the obstacle of the patients, reality was reestablished and stabilized. A firm and durable relationship bound me to Mama. Yet there was still a last obstruction to eliminate: the loss of reality during Mama's illness. In the beginning I thought she was ill deliberately in order to punish me. Then I experienced intense disturbance and a sensation of unreality each time she fell ill, and I did not know her. Finally, thanks to the fact that Mama had shown me my effectiveness in restoring her voice (during an attack of laryngitis)* I no longer felt impotent. Suddenly I found myself dominant over an illness, lending me courage to search for every applicable procedure in restoring Mama's missing voice. Soon I discovered that reality was rich in methods of curing illnesses—compresses, medicaments, gargles—a discovery making for even greater love and appreciation of reality and I grew more and more "adult" and independent of Mama.

With this victory, the consolidation of my grip on marvelous reality leaped with giant strides. Nonetheless, strangely enough, I could lose it from one moment to the next if, rarely, Mama was annoyed with me or if she upset me. Yet these little episodes intruded often enough to convince me that the integrity of reality depended entirely on my good relationship with Mama. She was the wellspring, the source of normal reality perception. She had only to alter her attitude toward me for living reality to be metamorphosed into a stage setting of arid desert. Even then, she had but to kiss me in reconciliation, and with a stroke of the magic wand, reality came again in life, warm, magnificent, vibrant, palpitating. The unpleasantness of other persons was futile in induc-

*Described in *La réalisation symbolique.*

ing the transmutation phenomenon. Equally when Mama's annoyance had brought it into being, no one but she could restore normality. For this reason I was zealous to maintain our good relationship, giving in at once lest anything disrupt it.

Meanwhile I succeeded in strengthening myself to such a point that at the end of two years I was able to oppose Mama and even—something unheard of—to defend myself when she chose to be annoyed with me. And without losing reality! In the matter of stable and valid perception, I had become independent.

I still had to fix the limits of my personality. For example, in my first attempt to secure a distant object, I had signaled with my hand and was impatient if it did not come to me. There followed a long learning period until I began to understand that it was I who had to do the moving. This was equally true in body functions. When I urinated and it was raining torrents outside, I was not at all certain whether it was not my own urine bedewing the world, and I was gripped by fear.

A comparable problem was posed with Mama. Sometimes I did not know clearly whether it was she or I who needed something. For instance if I asked for another cup of tea and Mama answered teasingly, "But why do you want more tea; don't you see that I have just finished my cup and so you don't need any?" Then I replied, "Yes, that's true, I don't need any more," confusing her with myself. But at bottom I did desire a second cup of tea and I said, "But I still want some more tea," and suddenly, in a flash, I realized the fact that Mama's satiety did not make me sated too. And I was ashamed to let myself be thus trapped by Mama and to watch her laugh at my discomfiture.

Confusion of this sort occurred frequently. Nor do I quite know whom it concerned, Mama or me, or me or Mama. Another thing that happened often was the dissociation of myself from any painful part of my body. For example, if I had a toothache, I went to Mama and said, "There's a tooth of mine that's cutting up. Talk to it." And Mama would say, "Tooth, are you going to leave my little Renee alone? Mama orders it. You will take the medicine I am going to give you and let my Renee sleep. You understand, tooth?" and I answered for the tooth, "Yes, Mama."

This personification of the painful parts of my body was a great boon. For when something hurt, I experienced a disagreeable sense of injury, even of attack, on my personality. To me, the pain was an intrusion, a stranger, and at the same time I had pity for the ill part and allied myself with Mama, on one hand, to banish the trouble which prevented my sleeping and, on the other, to care for and to commiserate with the painful area.

Little by little, meanwhile, I began to see the pain as a natural phenomenon belonging to reality and no longer deriving from a magical origin. And the oneness of my body and myself was conclusively accomplished.

What remained longest and was difficult to eliminate was the habit I had of saying, "I am afraid of the wolf," or "of *Die Polizei*" (the police), words I uttered whenever I dreaded something or was in great distress. Actually when I said, "I am afraid of the wolf" or "of the police," I did not imagine either a wolf or the police for I was afraid of neither one nor the other. Therefore when people wanted to quiet me, asserting that there was no wolf and that they would protect me from the police, I was not at all reassured. These two expressions were nothing but vague improvisations to express the fear. The "wolf" was something large and black, crying, "hou, hou," and gave rise to anxiety. But I neither saw nor thought of a wolf. Mama alone understood the diffuse panic hidden behind these phrases drained of sense and symbolism. She comforted me, saying, "Why are you so afraid, nothing is going to happen to you; Mama is here to watch. Did you think of something that frightened you?" And most of the time she was right; I had thought for an instant that Mama might die; then I had forgotten the thought, but the disquiet remained. Mama's question defined the idea generating the anxiety; then the anxiety itself disappeared.

These small phenomena, however, were nothing compared with what I had long undergone. In their turn, they too vanished.

If I can put it that way, reality became more real, more rich, and I more social and independent. Now I can accept Mrs. Sechehaye in her own right. I love her for herself and I am enternally grateful to her for the priceless treasure she has granted me in restoring reality and contact with Life.

Only those who have lost reality and lived for years in the Land of cruel, inhuman Enlightenment can truly taste the joy in living and prize the transcendent significance of being a part of humanity.

PART II

INTERPRETATION

Stages in Ego Disintegration

17 With a remarkable capacity for introspection, Renee has related the personal experiences of her inner life during her illness. These experiences raise numerous problems, all of them of unusual interest: the problem of the break into schizophrenia; of the perception of reality in the mentally ill; of the relationship between delirium and hallucination, to name only a few. Only one will be considered here, which, though correlated with the others, appears to be the most vital: the problem of the ego.

Quite unlike the situation in neurosis, schizophrenia seems to be primarily an ego sickness. Certainly in the psychotic, there is an eruption of unconscious life into the field of consciousness, an encroachment possible only in the face of ego-breakdown.

In a previous work on symbolic realization, the importance of primary drives in the psychological origin of psychosis was indicated, particularly the importance of oral and aggressive drives. They will not be discussed here specifically; nonetheless these drives must be kept constantly in mind, for it is from them that the ego draws energized material in the elaboration of delirious and hallucinatory symptoms.

If before her illness certain sectors of Renee's ego had remained in the infantile phase, the cause lies in fixation at the weaning period. Compelled to renounce the mother in reality, this intolerable sacrifice is compensated by becoming, so to say, her own mother in imagination, that is, by withdrawing into autism. Not having accepted the emotional weaning, the model for all subsequent sacrifices, Renee's ego could never attain the degree of oblativity necessary to social living. For this reason, at the age of adult responsibility it would expose a vulnerability favorable to the psychotic break-through.

So vast and so complex is the psychological problem of the ego that only those definite points lending themselves to study and verification in Renee's case will be considered. Discussion will center on two phases: the disintegration of the ego by the illness, and its reconstruction according to a system utilizing symbolic realization.

Development of the Pathological Perception of Reality

Renee's introspection reveals that the earliest disturbing subjective symptom bears uniquely on the perception of reality. Suddenly objects become enormous, cut off, detached, without relation to one another; space appears limitless and anxiety supervenes. This phenomenon of strangeness, of unreality is at first circumscribed, then progressively extends to the perception of objects, of people, of herself. That this progression coincides perfectly with the aggravation of the illness is clear, for Renee compares the psychotic condition into which she has fallen with the state of total unreality partially experienced when her illness first began.

How can this phenomena, so painful for the victim, be explained, a phenomenon characterized by the detachment of objects, by the impression of immensity, of cinematography? Presumably, the causes of these strange impressions can be found in the ego itself.

An energy imbalance is manifest in the

ego. Those sectors formerly in contact with certain objects are no longer nourished by libidinal energy. They lack life and warmth. In the incipient stages, only some areas of the ego are attacked, accounting for Renee's experience of strangeness only on specific occasions: at school, on the street, in those circumstances having social implications. For the first portions of the ego to regress are precisely those closely related to society. Their energy, the libido, drains back to the innermost core of the ego, leaving the social sectors void of affect. As a result, the feeling of strangeness can be regarded as the earliest sign of ego disintegration: Renee has lost synthesis and perspective.

Normally the world of objects is perceived on a relative scale, each thing in its allotted space, coordinated by angles of vision. Each object is perceived in its relation to another, and in relation to the ground on which it stands. Further, a utilitarian function is attributed to seen objects: a chair is used to sit on. When, however, particular areas of the ego have been drained of energy, objects no longer appear in inter-individual relationships. The spaces separating and arranging them on different planes are eliminated. This is why each object appears as a whole in itself, cut away, detached, larger than life, and why space seems limitless, without depth or control, without the successive planes lending a third dimension. This bizarre reality-perception is the intellectual aspect of loss of ego-synthesis.

But this feeling of strangeness has an affective basis of which the accompanying anxiety is an unmistakable indication. Renee apparently experiences the sense of unreality whenever contact with the mother analyst is broken. Aggression against the mother is then the principal causal factor.

The loss of the real derives from two closely related sources. On the one hand, in the state of disintegration into which the ego has fallen, Renee is no longer master of a stable universe distinct from her inner world, a universe where the mother plays a part as a person. The mother is only the patient's extension of herself, the one who satisfies her needs. When, then, this image fails to satisfy the needs, the mother cannot be recognized. On the other hand, what seems to be the mother-analyst's unwillingness to relieve the primordial need provokes violent aggression resulting in an immediate break in the affective contact. However, since it dares not project itself on the loved object, the aggression returns to its point of departure: the ego conditions a strong sense of guilt inherent in the affective realism.

In addition to the aggression, another

cause basic to the impression of loss of reality lies in the reluctance to accept the mother as a social and autonomous being. For what is the social mother if not reality itself?

Because Renee cannot accept the social mother she breaks with reality. Certain segments of the ego are emptied of libidinal energy, the very source of life. The areas of the ego remaining sound experience the assault of unreality and struggle against it. For even a partial loss of reality contact engenders a profound sense of insecurity and abandonment related closely to the atmosphere of a nightmare.

Defense Mechanisms of the Psychotic Ego

As Renee outlines the sequence in the evolution of her illness, it becomes apparent that for larger and larger sectors of the ego the lines demarking reality become blurred to a degree producing a chaos of confusion between the ego and the non-ego, or what Baldwin calls an "adualism."

The imbalance between assimilation in the ego itself and accommodation to reality augments constantly; Renee no longer retains awareness of her subjectivity. Lacking this capacity for clear awareness of inner impressions, she projects them on the outside world. Inner components like suffering, fear and aggression, little by little are attributed to inanimate objects or to physical movements seemingly analogous to inner activity. The outside universe is progressively transformed in relation to the ego through inability to localize in consciousness those impressions already felt.

But this breaking through of inner components into the outer world stems as well from the intensity and violence of the impressions already experienced. Primary drives terrify an ego no longer in condition to resist them. In its weakness it utilizes the only mechanism for defense at its disposal—projection. This is the "animistic" period of the illness, reminiscent of the phase through which childhood thinking evolves, a process masterfully described by Piaget.

The scenes that take place around her are now undissociated from the patient's inner world; nor is the ego independent in its own right, but is broken up in the objects themselves. It is for this reason that Renee hears her own protest, her own suffering and hostility in the sigh of the wind and the rustling of trees. "Isn't the wind carrying a message of misfortune?" Soon she believes the wind can destroy the earth.

One can scarcely apply the word "delirium" to this distortion of external facts in relation to the ego. Rather there is here one of the mechanisms of symbolic thinking, characteristic of schizophrenic regression and evident in the small child's thinking. Yet this attribution of inner components to the forces of nature, corresponding to the stirrings of the mind, actually constitutes the nucleus of subsequent delirium.

In proportion as Renee loses subjective self-awareness, she increasingly localizes her feelings in things. The boundaries separating the inner world of thinking from the outer world of reality shade off, then fade out. Objects are alive, they become threatening, they sneer, they torment her; they are invested with her own aggression harbored against the world. Only contact with the analyst momentarily relieves the suffering and allows her, in a small measure, to rediscover reality. (The writer had yet to come on the procedure utilizing symbolic realization, hence was unable to arrest the course of ego-disintegration.)

Shortly after, the unconscious erupts into Renee's ego in the form of aggressive impulses and an intense desire to return to the mother. The healthy area of the ego musters its strength to expel the intolerable unconscious drives: this is the elaboration of the delirium. Aggression and self-castigation are projected onto the "System," a machine designed to punish people and Renee herself. The patient no longer conceives her mental activity as inner and dependent on her own consciousness but localizes it in things. Disagreeable thoughts are experienced as echoes, as repetitions and as psychic hallucinations. In the same way, impulses toward mutilation and self-destruction are attributed to the "System."

However, as some sectors of the ego—unfortunately narrower and narrower—are still sound, they remain at the service of the instinct of self-preservation and refuse to obey the "System's" orders, accepted by the psychotic ego. According to Renee's story, there follows a dissociation translated into a painful aura of comedy, of artificiality, having nonetheless the effect of complete sincerity. This dualism will not disappear until the ego in its entirety has substituted an imaginary world for actual reality.

When Renee has regressed to this phase, she no longer maintains subjective awareness. This is why, henceforth, she regards herself, not as a person, but as a "personage," to whom one speaks in the third person. This new self-conception explains her relief when the analyst addresses her in the third person as one does a one or two year old child. The same phenomenon appears regarding the analyst whom Renee no longer recognizes as an individual in her own right, but only as Mama, as a personification of the Mama whom alone she loved and wanted.

Soon the boundaries dividing the ego from the id have crumbled and the disorganized eruption of aggression distorts perception. It is at this period, Renee says, that she began to place the "voices," as she called them, at the far corner of the room. With amazing introspection and sincerity, Renee confesses that she did not hear words, nor voices, nor whisperings, nor any kind of sound. Yet she behaved exactly as if she were beset by the most lively auditory hallucinations. How to explain this paradox? De Quercy, in his book *The Hallucination*, describes patients who seemingly experience hallucinations yet hear little, if anything; they are rather interpreting their own thoughts.

This does not seem to be true in the present instance. At this period the phenomenon of echo or of thought repetition was absent. She was annoyed by and responded to something sensorially nonexistent, but always localized in the same place. In this paradoxical phenomenon, there may exist a phase intermediate between psychic hallucination and true sensory hallucination. Psychologically, this phenomenon can be interpreted as an eruption of repressed material overwhelming the capacities of an ego in a state of disintegration.

Recognizing the unacceptable components in the eruption, the ego projects them outwards at once. Too shaken by the psychotic break-through, the ego has no time to elaborate these feelings, these unconscious tendencies, into a bearable, verbally symbolic form, into the thematic auditory hallucination with its familiar characteristics of spatial and sensory localization. The ego is overpowered: it casts out what horrifies it and is shocked at the exteriorized unconscious feelings. One might almost speak here of "unconscious hallucinations." Only later will the ego elaborate the repressed material in verbal expression and Renee will hear the voices in a truly sensory way. There will then be actual auditory hallucinations.

In the writer's *Symbolic Realization*, this process is described. Renee could not love herself since her mother had refused to nourish, hence love, her. When the ego is no longer charged with libidinal energy produced by the introjection of maternal love, destructive forces soon invade it. As Freud has shown, there is a complication of drives. When the libidinal drives are frustrated, the drives to self-preservation lose their defensive energy and abandon the ego to self-destruction. He sees in the latter one aspect of the death-instinct linked to primary masochism.

The destructive urges robbed Renee of the will to live and induced attempts at self-injury. At certain times her delirium even took on a tinge of melancholy.

The unbearable blameworthiness weighing so heavily on her cannot be ascribed to a cruel and punitive super-ego. Though these inherent feelings of guilt and self-punishment lie at the primary level of psychosymptomatology they constitute only a superstructure, epiphenomenal in nature. Actually, Renee's conflict operated entirely at the oral level, a level necessarily antedating the Oedipus when the superego comes into being. Here the question is one of primary guilt deriving from "affective realism," that new and important aspect of realism so well described by Odier of Lausanne in *Anxiety and Magical Thinking:* "Affective realism can be viewed as a vital aspect of the child's life causing him to imagine that all his joys and sorrows are determined by outside influences and that his good or ill fortune depends on the intervention of the beings and things that surround him."

Renee's prelogical reasoning followed this

sequence: "Mama does not feed me because she doesn't want to feed me. Consequently it is wicked to keep on wanting the mother-feeding that is denied me. To be angry about it is even more wicked." Following on this prelogical argument, the ego finds a proof of guilt in the self-destructive drives themselves. Finally the aggression against the bad-mother, which dares not manifest itself directly, turns automatically to the point of origin, the ego, further reinforcing the death impulses.

When the little monkey, her double, was ordered to keep his arms down, the impulses to self-harm disappeared. This fact emphasizes the relation existing between the destructive drives and the libido. By the mechanism of magical, presymbolic participation, the patient projects her drives on the little monkey which is, at the same time, Renee herself. For if the mother-analyst lowers the little monkey's arms, ordering him to keep them down, this means to Renee that her mother is opposed to what harms her, that her mother allows her to live. This proof of love, bestowed magically, and the only one the patient can understand, constitutes a narcissistic screen powerful enough to inhibit the death drives momentarily. Nevertheless it is to be expected that this development of exogenous protection relating to the magic act of lowering the monkey's arms is only a palliative.

Oral Sources of the Feeling of Reality

To deliver Renee from the tentacles of the basic drives, it was imperative to get at the activating causes rather than at their secondary results. Only when it became clear that the intense need for mother-feeding had to be satisfied could Renee be freed of the aggression and self-destruction.

In giving her at stated times a piece of apple, symbol of the maternal breast, the primal need was assuaged, a need persisting into adulthood and arresting the ego in a condition of deep regression. Feeling herself loved for the first time in the only way she could acknowledge, the magic way, Renee experienced a wonderful sense of reality which both amazed and delighted her. At a single stroke of the wand normal perception replaced morbid distortion. Instead of seeing things and people cut off, immense, isolated, unrelated, from then on they fell into normal proportions and into their inter-individual relationships. All reality was invested with the libidinal energy drawn from mother love; the world was warm, alive, affectively charged.

In their turn, delirium and hallucinations

vanished. But more particularly the dreadful anxiety, born of the disorganized emergence of unconscious drives into the impotent ego, gave way to a benign sense of security and protection: "I am loved!"

In short, the establishment of possible contact between Renee and the mother-analyst, even on the oral level alone, at once restored contact with reality. Is not the mother-nurse the earliest form of the non-ego? And is she not then the source of all subsequent reality?

New Trauma and Massive Regression of the Ego to the Fetal Phase

Unfortunately, at this time the method of symbolic realization was far from systematized and the writer made the error of trying too rapidly to make Renee independent of the mother-analyst. Abruptly the contact was broken. With the sudden departure of her nurse, reawaking the complex of abandonment, Renee endured additional trauma. One day, when she refused to eat, instead of insisting as should have been done, it was suggested that she might leave her dinner if she wasn't hungry. Renee interpreted these words as an order by her mother not to eat, in other words, not to live. A violent crisis shook her to the depths and again the self-destructive forces took the upper hand, the love of the mother-nurse being no longer present to protect the ego against invasion. Renee fell, as she recounts it, into a state well this side of any thought or speech. The regression consequent on this crisis carried her back to the most primitive level, the fetal stage.

Her sole desire was to return to her mother's body, a desire whose achievement could lie only in suicidal attempts. Given up completely to these death impulses, the disintegrated ego had no more strength to rebuild the pathological structure it had elaborated. So it was that the delirium and hallucinations, reappearing once more, lost all emotional quality, all trace of thematic outline, and were reduced to stereotypes, to verbal perseverations and automatisms. Participating no longer in the structural effort of the psychotic ego, emotions were degraded to the grossest and most violent level. All the signs at this period pointed to a swift descent to the affective dementia which she revealed when she began to speak her "language."

The term "language," however, is hardly appropriate as a translation of what actually was the case. The phonemes used by Renee were no more than a few syllables, and always the same: "ichtiou, raite, ovede, gao," etc., having none of the characteristics proper to a true verbal sign or even to a symbol. To linguists, the sign is a meaningful optional linked by social convention to what it stands for; while the symbol is a meaning having a resemblance to what it stands for (i.e., a metaphor). There was nothing of either of these in Renee's language. No conceptual or affective meaning (in the symbolic sense) was inherent in these phonemes nor could they be considered as verbal schemes, to use Piaget's terminology, where the child applies an onomatopoeia (waou) to all kinds of different things; for in the verbal scheme there exists, primitive though it may be, a subjective bond between the phonemes uttered by the child and objects or actions, whereas in Renee's case, no relation with objects or actions could be discerned. These syllables constituted a verbal expression of the most primary sort, issuing directly from the unconscious and having all the characteristics of the symbol: unawareness, extreme mobility in relation to the fixity of the sign and sensory-motor imitation. They might be seen as unconscious manifestations, the protests and wishes of the small child, and at the same time as a participation in the reassuring and consoling maternal voice. From this it is obvious to what a regressed state Renee's ego had returned.

Stages in Ego Reconstruction

18 It has been possible to trace step by step the ego's route toward psychotic disintegration. From the analytic point of view it might be concluded that the continuous regression had led the ego beyond the oral to the fetal stage. In every disintegrative phenomenon, according to Jackson's theory, a positive and negative aspect must be distinguished, both illustrated in the arrival at the terminal stage. Negatively, Renee had sought a return to the mother through repeated suicidal attempts; positively, through retreat to complete autism.

Symbolic Realization of the Fetal Phase as the
Beginning of Ego Reconstruction

During the fetal stage of regression, the writer determined to attempt contact with the patient. By then, thanks to numerous experiences with Renee, the certainty was clear that if the method were to succeed it was absolutely vital to consider the level of regression and not exceed it unless the patient herself signified willingness.

Needless to say, at the fetal stage to which Renee had slipped, the ego no longer existed as a conscious entity; the confusion between the ego and the non-ego was complete so that no participation could be expected from her. Furthermore at this period she seemed not even to recognize the analyst; nonetheless an effort was made to create some bond, tenuous though it might be, capable of re-establishing contact. This could be accomplished only by satisfying the need inherent in the current phase of regression.

Therefore, when Renee indicated a desire to return to the mother's body, it was critical to aid and not oppose her in the realization of her wish. Thus far only the negative aspect had been sanctioned; that is, she had been protected against her suicidal attempts by straightjackets and padded walls. Henceforth, a support of the positive aspect would permit escape into any degree of autism.

Further, she would be convinced that she might return to the maternal body and that the satisfaction of her desire depended directly on the mother-analyst. In this way the almost physiological craving to be placed symbolically in the "green sea," as she called it, was gratified.

Because of her kidney ailment Renee suffered severe physical pain, necessitating frequent morphine injections. Formerly these had been left either to the physician or the nurse, and when the writer undertook their administration, no other meaning than of a simple physical ministration was assigned to it. However, the repose provided by the sedative offered the opportunity to satisfy Renee's need. One day when the suffering was acute and she tried in every way to bite and strike herself, she was told, "Mama doesn't want Renee to suffer; Mama wants Renee to go into the green sea." Then the injection was administered. While the drug was taking effect, the hangings were drawn and the room thrown into green shadow. "You see, Mama has placed Renee in the green sea; now she can relax." A faint smile, the first in a long time, passed over her face, and she fell asleep, relaxed and at peace.

When next Renee was in pain and cried, "The green, the green has gone," in the same way the "green sea" was restored and she was granted authoritative maternal permission to remain altogether passive, to enjoy the perfect serenity of the unborn child, thus creating a bond, elementary perhaps, between the patient and the mother-analyst. Forced to recognize Mama as the source of her satisfaction her attention was directed outward and a link forged with the environment.

Renee was now ready for ego reconstruction. Certainly at the fetal stage there was no question of an autonomous ego. Nonetheless, in gratifying her need, her attention had been directed outward to the source of her pleasure, stimulating an expectation, an awareness of its dynamism. Up to this time, everything had been confusion, disintegration, agitation, the necessity to return to the mother not yet dissociated from self-destructive impulses. Then Renee discovered certain relationships—still global—between her own desire and the object of its satisfaction. She learned that when she cried, "The sea is no longer there, Renee wants the green," she was again restored to it, to the "sea," by the hypodermic injection (when she was better, solely by the artificial twilight in her room). In this way, a causality was established, a causality still primitive since she did not dissociate the efficacy from its phenomenal quality.

At this stage, the mother is no more than the focus of the patient's wants. But to the degree that this function was repeated in the same pleasant way, Renee began to dissociate the two aspects of the relation: she conceived the mother-analyst as the center of action and ascribed to her the effective origins of her pleasure. Until that time she had depended on herself to conjure up the "green sea," crying and calling for it. Now she understood that her satisfaction came from without.

When she was physically well and injections were no longer necessary, she was placed in the "sea" simply by darkening the room. Her need having been assuaged, the guilt occasioned by her desire to enter the mother's body over the latter's objection disappeared. From this time on, the patient could fix on the object, the source of her pleasure, and she began to enjoy the mother's presence without the urgency to enter into her. This represented great progress.

To continue on this road it was necessary to utilize this valuable insight, namely, that the first attention the patient gives to the outside world derives from the gratification of the primal need.

Creation of the New "Imago"

The primary objective at this point was the achievement of an image of herself, a new "imago" on which Renee could construct an ego. At the level to which she had regressed, merely corporeal and affective impressions existed without yet possessing any awareness of subjective activity, for which reasons the mechanism of projection, an essentially unconscious mechanism, was utilized.

The doll (first Moses, then Ezekiel) cared for by the mother with the liveliest solicitude, tenderly kissed, rocked and cuddled, became for Renee a model on which her unconscious ego could project itself. Actually, people and things were but an extension of herself, yet something other than herself. This mechanism clearly involves presymbolic magical participation, presupposing a complete unconsciousness of self. For a while, Renee was content to stand passively by during the care of Ezekiel, enjoying it by proxy. Meanwhile it became easier to feed her, particularly if Ezekiel was given the "breast" before her meal. Then one day Renee made bold to push Ezekiel's head against the analyst's bosom with her own hand, watching attentively for any reaction. By this gesture she established a more intimate relationship between her ego and its symbol, between what was signified and its sign. And when she was reassured that Ezekiel was to be fed regularly, she agreed readily from then on to feed herself.

Until now only a complete lack of differentiation between the ego and its designated symbol could be observed. But to the degree that Renee's unconscious felt secure in the mother-analyst's love, the energy thus far subserving the self-destructive impulses was liberated for transfer to the instinct of ego-preservation. From this moment Renee began, albeit only on the oral level, to distinguish herself from the symbol, to accept for herself the food given to Ezekiel. Nevertheless the symbol as such was not relinquished.

Imitative Process in the Service of Ego Formation

By the use of Ezekiel, a new "imago" was elaborated, the "imago" of a happy child loved by its mother. At this time Renee began to adopt a new form of behavior complementary to the earlier, a behavior allowing her gradually to reconstruct the ego and organized about the imitative process.

Baldwin conceives imitation as one of two sources yielding self-awareness and awareness of others; the other is projection.

According to him, the infant comes to self-consciousness in imitating the behavior of those around him. Piaget, in his excellent study *Symbol Formation in the Child*, presents the genesis and evolution of imitation in six phases. If he particularly emphasizes the close relationship between the evolution of imitation and the evolution of intelligence, he lays stress also, but more implicitly, on imitation in its relation to the growth of self-awareness. In the earliest phases, the child imitates only those movements which it can execute spontaneously, without, however, consequent adaptation to new models.

Transposed to the affective level, this can be assumed applicable to Renee. By means of projection, Renee could eat alone, copying herself as she copied Ezekiel, her symbol, first projecting her own needs on the doll, then imitating whatever he reproduced of her own behavior.

Piaget observed this phenomenon in the twelve-to-eighteen month-old infant who projects his own eating and drinking behavior on animals, then imitates them in turn. This evolutionary phase of the symbol Piaget called "the stage of projection of imitation schemata." In the infant, the element of play occupies the principal role in projection phenomena. Of the greatest interest in the study of the schizophrenic ego is the similarity between the construction of the infantile ego and the reconstruction of the psychotic ego. From the phenomenologic and structural points of view, both pass through identical phases, but from the functional angle they differ fundamentally.

Early in the genesis of Renee's ego, she had but imitated her double, reproducing her own behavior previously projected on the doll. In the second period this imitation changed, evidence of considerable progress over the preceding phase, for to reproduce the desired deportment already projected on its symbol implies no further accommodation to the object. Imitation is confused with assimilation and presymbolic magical participation.

In the second period Renee takes the mother-analyst as a model for imitation which now takes on a truly independent function. But it is clear that if Renee begins to imitate the mother, the latter is not then copied as an autonomous being, regardless of her activities, but solely in relation to the patient's primary needs, in this instance confined strictly to the feeding area.

Instead of remaining passive, Renee now begins to imitate the mother-nurse. Therefore at mealtimes she repeats every word and copies every gesture. For example, if, stroking her cheek, the mother-analyst says, "Drink your milk, my dear," Renee gravely repeats the phrase several times with the same stress and intonation, stroking her own cheek the while. At this time the imitation is sensory-motor, implying a confusion of her own ego with that of the mother-analyst. The incessant repetition of phrases can be accounted for by the assimilation process and the establishment of the imitated behavior. Renee now also imitates certain interesting movements to stimulate their repetition as though she attributes to her gesture alone a causal and effective meaning operating to inspire activities in the mother.

To illustrate: when Renee wishes to be covered, she several times pretends to spread a blanket, staring fixedly meanwhile at the analyst, an action serving to instigate the desired behavior or to have the desired behavior reproduced by the cherished object. It is apparent that this behavior conforms singularly with Piaget's description of the nine-month-old infant's "effective techniques" or "techniques for continuing an interesting spectacle." As with the baby, at this level Renee's activities are not objectified but centered entirely on herself.

Nevertheless, once the copy of the model has been fixed by repetition, the imitation is by degrees detached from the model. To use

Piaget's terminology again, there is the appearance of a "delayed imitation," an imitation consequently independent of the analyst's presence. By the imitative gesture alone the absent object is evoked, indicating Renee's new capacity for exact reproduction of voice and movements when she is separated from the model. She treats herself as she has been treated but is not content to copy while remaining herself; instead she becomes one with the model, and is herself her own mother. Here again is a similarity to Piaget's infant in that the imitative gesture plays the symbolizing role, the imitated individual the symbolized role. In the fusion of real imitation and its assimilation in the ego, these two phenomena coalesce.

The appearance of this new capacity for imitating an absent model is of the greatest significance in ego development, indicating as it does the beginning of maternal introjection. The model no longer remains outside the ego but is progressively interiorized. Nonetheless it is still necessary that some physical bond with the model reinforce the mental image of the mother, that the latter share in the imitation by an intermediary deriving directly from her. For this reason, while she eats alone Renee must hold in her hand a paper on which have been written certain words addressed to her. These she reads and repeats many times. Soon the paper is no longer indispensable, the model is conclusively interiorized, evidence that the ego is beginning its structural organization. It cannot yet be said that Renee is aware of having an ego like her mother's or anyone else's, for even though she no longer confuses herself completely with the loved mother, equivalent to a degree of dissociation from her, she still speaks to herself in the third person and regards herself as a "personage," announcing before and during meals, "Renee is drinking her milk; Mama has given Renee the milk," as though she were speaking of someone else. This is the assertive phase, to use Janet's terminology, when the subject sees himself as a personage. This stage Pichon calls "the built-out person" in distinction to the "spare person," when the "I-me" concept develops. According to this, the "built-out person" represents the collection of differentiating characteristics, the "spare person" the irreducible and permanent core of the personality, the "I." In Renee the "built-out person" does not have the generality ascribed to it by Pichon, but represents a specific entity centered about the oral; she might rather be called an "oral person."

As Freud has shown, the incessant repetition of each phrase has the function of establishing a solid bond between past and present data, of reinforcing assimilation schemata. In this case it operates to bind closely the person of Renee and the imitated mother inasmuch as she adds to "Renee drinks her milk," the indispensable phrase, "Mama gives it to Renee."

Personality structure is still in the participation period. Soon, by means of the repetition technique which strengthens the interiorization of the model and affectively keeps the loved mother for herself, the patient attains a new level, the level of mother introjection with its implication of subjective awareness. As Baldwin has said, imitation is at once the source of the *ego* and of the *alter ego*, achieving gradual awareness of itself as the child copies the actions of others. Analogously, in reflecting her mother, Renee has become conscious of herself, with the consequent immediate appearance of the "I." Soon she announces, "*I* am drinking my milk, Mama gives it to *me.*" Yet she still finds it necessary to fortify the introjection by interpolating the word mother and the objective "Mama gives it to me." A last remnant of verbal participation persists but soon tends to disappear.

It is only when she has completely identified herself with her mother that Renee is satisfied to say, "I am drinking." She has become independent on the oral level. From the core of her ego has risen this sole instance, essentially specific and singular, the "I" marking the awareness of the irreducible and permanent in the diverse contents of the ego. It is equally awareness of will and freedom, proving that the ego is now endowed with structure and has finished the oral construction. Renee is no longer a personage but a person, a being. And so the progressive reconstruction of the ego is effected by the double technique of projection on Ezekiel and imitation of the mother-analyst, one complementing the other.

Construction of the Body Ego

Meanwhile, though Renee was developing an autonomous ego on the oral level, she was still not clearly cognizant of having a body, of being a body. For the ego is equally a body ego and by some modern thinkers is conceived as essentially body-awareness. Piaget points out that in proportion as the infant gains consciousness of himself, "desubjectivizes himself," he becomes mindful of a mobile body set in an immobile space, comprehending other bodies and interrelationships with them.

To arrive at the idea of being one among moving beings, performing in common necessitates a complete operative construction at the same time intellectual and affective. Like a small child, Renee did not imagine herself one with her own body, as proof of which she referred to her body as to an object independent of, though linked to, her; and when any part ailed, she at once objectified it, isolating it from the rest. As a result, she did not say, "My arm hurts," but "the arm is sick," quite as though it were an independent thing, thereby removing the arm as far from her body as possible. For the same reason she liked to hear, "What a nice body Renee has, how clean it is!" or she would announce, "There is a tooth cutting up; say something to it." When the author admonished the tooth, "Will you be good and leave my little Renee alone!" Renee identified herself with the tooth, answering "Yes, Mama; yes, Mama." This malleability of the ego simultaneously dissociating and identifying itself with an ailing organ indicates how little the structuration process achieved on the oral level holds together in the general personality scheme. It shows too how important is the awareness of being a body for a true synthesis of the ego to come about. The child's lack of recognition that he is one body among others stems uniquely from the imcompleteness of his intellectual evolution, while for Renee it was due to ego-disintegration and to the withdrawal of the libido from its object. She could not love her body as long as it was unloved by the mother-analyst. It had to be admired, dressed attractively, to convince her of this love and of her right to love it in turn. As in eating, she adopted both mechanisms of projection and imitation. She began by wanting beautiful clothes and zealous care for Ezekiel; then she copied the mother's activities in relation to her own body objectified in the doll. Later she imitated gestures, complimentary words relative to herself. Finally she reproduced words and gestures without the necessity of a model. Imitation on the narcissistic level was interiorized, implying introjection of the mother. The model actuated an image with a life of its own, inspiring imitation. At this stage, Renee no longer objectified her body; insensible of it, she made one with it. When her teeth or feet hurt her, she said, "I have a toothache," "My foot hurts," just as she said, "I am washing."

Affective Bases in the Structuration of the Real

Even though Renee was now aware of being "a body," she had yet to acquire a feeling of bodily relationships, a conception of her body in immobile space among other bodies. In short she had not yet reached what logicians call "the logic of relations," since she still measured the position and displacements of objects in relation to herself. Therefore, when she wished to determine a point in spatial orientation, without much concern for precise objective relationships, she could say, "In front of me the north, behind me the south, at my right the east, at my left the west," quite as though she were an animated map. She was amazed that the cardinal directions were as mobile and variable as the position of her body; for, in executing a half-turn to the right, what had been the north became the west while the west was located on her left.

This illustrates to what degree geometric egocentrism still operated. Still confined in her personal angle of vision, the spatial sense was yet to be elaborated and structured. The same egocentrism prevented comprehension of perspective, as, for example, when during a motor trip the mountain seen from a distance lost its identity on closer approach. Reassured that it was the same, she asked, "But it is changed. Why has it taken this shape?"

This regressed stage bears a marked resemblance to Piaget's descriptions in *The Child's Construction of Reality*, in which he attributes the inadequate spatial-temporal structuration to an operative evolution in process of construction. It is interesting to note, however, that an affective regression may produce the same phenomena. In Renee's case, a gradual building of a perceived universe will come about in relation to her affective development. For Renee to arrive at a "logic of relations," she must establish interpersonal relations between her ego and the mother-analyst, the chosen and representative object of reality. Toward this end it was imperative that she attain the essential idea of the *constant identity of the mother*, whom until now she had seen only as "mother," the extension of herself, united with herself. For this reason, because she had not yet libidinally invested the social sectors of the maternal personality, she lost reality. She could no longer recognize the mother-analyst nor maintain contact with her when the latter was ill, when she received guests or went shopping.

To the degree, however, that magical symbolic realization satisfied her unconscious needs, the initial ego-centrism diminished, allowing the ego to take account of other persons' opinions. As she herself reported, the fact that she could restore "Mama's" voice during an attack of laryngitis enabled her on one hand to accept the illness, and on the other to discover a remedy in reality. In this painful situation where she was unable to recognize the mother's new aspect Renee could accept it only by gradual assimilation and on the symbolic level of other familiar situations. Realizing her ability to restore the lost voice by invoking it, she henceforth no longer feared her mother's escaping her since now she knew her power in bringing her back at will.

By the animistic process, terror of the unknown disappeared and Renee was able to establish a bond between the known and unknown mother, the mother as an individual. By grace of the magic act, the reassured ego could now summon into reality the behavior suitable to restoring the voice; she prepared throat compresses and inhalations, ran through drug lists in search of the most effective—in short, acted the true nurse. In this way, the ever more important areas of the mother-analyst's personality were recognized and incorporated in the ego. On this level Renee learned to accept the analyst in her varied social capacities, as the mistress of the house receiving guests, the shopper in stores and the like. In each of these activities, she could establish a relationship between the nurse-mother and the social-mother.

As a matter of fact, the first guests were

the nurse whom she loved, then a little girl who interested her, then her doctor; the first purchases she watched were things for herself or things she gave away and she was thus at the origin of these activities. Soon she recognized the analyst in situations independent of herself. All that remained was the acceptance of a professional analyst receiving patients to whom she had transferred the accumulated aggression against her brothers and sisters. Here, too, there operated the symbolic realization of her unconscious need, permitting her first to accept the author's concern with patients, then to accept tolerantly their presence, and finally to become interested in them and the analyst herself. The latter's individual and social personality was conclusively recognized and incorporated in the ego, thus lending a permanent identity.

Consequent on this, improvement was striking. In establishing relationships between her ego and the social mother, Renee traveled far on the road to the "logic of relations." She no longer considered everything in terms of her own actions, but saw herself as one person among others having the same rights and duties as herself. In proportion to this gradual decentralization and the concomitant assimilation of reality by the ego, Renee began increasingly to differentiate inner impressions from the world outside. For this reason magical-animistic and magical-artefactious behavior disappeared, yielding to the socially fitting. The adjustment of the libido to the outer world and to people and reciprocal relations between the ego and others were reestablished, as were the barriers separating the ego from reality. In elaborating the ego Renee simultaneously elaborated her universe and she evolved slowly and surely to oblativity and adult objectivity. The ego, invested with libidinal energy and nourished by maternal love, was now fit to love itself and to live independent of the mother, itself adequately structured to structure the real and adapt to it. In particular, it was able to invest things and people with affectivity so well that, from a perception of the world syncretic, rigid and desolate, Renee ascended to a joyous vision of reality, alive, palpitant, proportionate.

Conclusions

Value of Symbolic Realization in Formative Mechanism of the Ego

In this study, confined to the examination of the psychotic ego, Renee's recital has permitted penetration beyond the hermetic symbolism related to delirium, to hallucinations and to schizophrenic behavior, so baffling in their ambivalence and dissociation. The phenomenologic and psychoanalytic exploration of the latency period, of ego-encroachment and of the stage of schizophrenic psychosis has demonstrated without ambiguity the really extraordinary importance of the role of *frustration* in ego disintegration. To it might be ascribed the initial ego weakness by virtue of which the psychosis is able to break through.

Once started in life with an unsatisfied basic need, Renee could make no adequate adaptation to reality. Approaching adulthood, a too-demanding environmental complexity drove her back to a lower, infantile level of development. The first sign of ego regression consisted in the strange perception of the real, giving rise to severe anxiety. As the illness effects disintegration the universe loses its spatial structure until it is replaced by another, essentially subjective and unstable. This progressive loss of reality stems from the withdrawal of libidinal energy brought about by the ego in support of the elaboration of delirium and hallucinations. By dint of the symbolic realization of her need for nourishment, once more Renee suddenly experiences the hitherto lost sense of reality. This temporary emergence of reality contact in the course of a fullblown psychosis seems to prove that regressions maintain a certain dynamism and are not as crystalized as might be supposed.

Meanwhile, due to the lack of systematization of the symbolic realization method and the errors this entailed, Renee sank to the last stages of collapse, involving a massive regression to the fetal level, a collapse rich in educational implications from the point of view both of the ego and of the inherent drives. Indeed, under cover of personality disintegration, it has been possible to study the mechanisms serving in ego reconstruction, mechanisms which in themselves possess no energizing strength and take on value only after the basic needs have been satisfied. It was necessary to compensate for the initial frustration by setting Renee in the "green sea," by authorizing her to assuage the desire to return to the mother. In relation to this symbolic satisfaction, the patient could again lend attention to reality, and through the mother-analyst, source of the satisfaction, accept benign reality.

Actually this assimilation of the objective world to one's own desire can hardly be called reality. Nevertheless it was the first link binding Renee to other people. At this time, the self-destructive impulses created by the frustration were neutralized by the libidinal tendencies drawn from maternal love, allowing the formative mechanisms of the ego to begin activity.

The similarity of the process of personality reconstruction and of the development of the small child is striking. Both utilize projection and imitation, the former first since it presupposes ego unawareness. Because Renee's ego was still unstructured she readily projected her needs and desires on the doll Ezekiel. Once assured of the mother's love she could adopt imitation, the more evolved second mechanism, and pass through all the stages of imitation traversed by the small child until the work of introjection and identification was completed. But, as has been seen, the ego could accomplish its synthesis only when body awareness had been achieved. The consciousness of "being a body" seems indispensable to the differentiation of the ego and non-ego. For is it not on the body that perceptions impinging on consciousness depend? Since it constitutes at once part of both subject and object, the body serves the function of linking the ego to the outer world, then to others.

Since Renee had no sensibility of "being a body" she distinguished with difficulty her own experiences and those of the outer world. As she herself says, when she urinated while it rained outside, she wondered suddenly if she could check the falling waters and was seized with anguish at her impotence. Toward distant things her reaction was similar. Instead of rising to fetch the thing she needed, she signaled with her hand and awaited its coming; in the face of the object's inertia she was amazed that it was she and not it that had to move.

In the same way if someone kissed her and asked for a kiss in return, she said, "But who did the kissing, you or I?" Or when she wanted something to drink and the answer was teasing, "But I am not thirsty," she quite failed to see the humor and replied resignedly, "Oh, yes, I am not thirsty any more." This behavior had occurred during a convalescence free of any psychotic manifestations, indicating that the body had not yet acquired its concomitant functions of linking and separating the ego and the outer world.

Louis Lavelle, Bergson's eminent successor, summarizes this phenomenon succinctly: "It is for this reason that the ego is nothing without its own body and without an awareness of the universe which would be impossible except for the body. Not that the body produces it [the ego] by a mysterious epiphenomenon, but in order for consciousness to exist, we must differentiate ourselves from the world and consequently realize our body limitations." For Renee to acquire this idea, critical in the formation of consciousness, it was essential that she be freed of the affective realism weighing on her and constituting an impenetrable superstructure of intense guilt. In effect the lack of maternal love had prevented the development of normal narcissism. Where then shall the personality derive the love of self lending it assurance and confidence in itself if not from introjected mother love? Here again the association of a vital drive (the self-preservation instinct) and the libido comes into question.

Now that Renee possessed a normal self-preservation instinct based on the satisfaction of her need for food, it remained to provide her with a normal libido. Again it was necessary to resort to the mechanisms of projection and imitation: the projection of her desires (to have a pretty body, to admire it and care for it) on the doll Ezekiel; the imitation of the mother-analyst's attitude first toward the body of the doll symbol, then to that of Renee herself.

At the moment when the affective realism is completely dissolved by the work of introjection and of identification with the loving mother, ego-synethesis is actually accomplished. The entire energy potential hitherto consumed in those factors comprising the psychosis is placed at the disposal of the ego. It is then possible to arrange a normal hierarchy of drives and to invest reality with the available libido. Instead of raising defense mechanisms against the invasion of drives and denying a too painful reality, the free and autonomous ego will adjust itself increasingly to the outer world, thereby terminating the essential function of symbolism and imitation, so critical in the reconstruction of the ego. This does not imply that they disappear without trace. On the contrary, the importance of their role in ego-genesis insures an integration in a new affective-intellectual personality structure.

In actuality, the symbol which originally served as a substitute for the object with which it was associated will change to an image, then into a concept. Thinking in images was a characteristic phase in Renee's evolution. In proportion, however, as she establishes social relations, first with the mother-analyst, then with other people, she will avail herself less and less of thinking by symbol and image, a type of thinking primarily self-centered, and resort to operative concepts. On the linguistic level the symbol is converted into a social sign, conventional or arbitrary (according to De Saussure's definition) and on the affective level into lasting self-identity and differentiation of others.

Imitation, once only a simple replica of the object, will gradually free itself of perception to become representation and in turn release the image of the absent mother. As Renee continues to dissociate with increasing nicety what belongs to the ego from what belongs to the non-ego, she will become aware of the imitations. At this stage imitation has become deliberate, integrated with intelligence and affectivity and placed at their disposal.

In a manner more complex and operative, the extension of these two mechanisms accompanies a new capacity to seize and structure the world of objects and ideas. As a solid and lasting universe elaborates, an aptitude for reasoning with the adult instruments of logical categories and relations makes its appearance, as does a comprehension of intellectual activity. From now on Renee can find an interest in science, especially in botany where she can utilize her craving for truth and objectivity, primary requisites in scientific research.

On the social plane, conscious of her personal autonomy as distinct from that of others, Renee can relate her thinking with others and work with them. The more mindful she is of her inner life, the more apt she becomes in putting herself in the place of others and understanding them. From the emotional standpoint she must overcome a developmental hurdle, the Oedipus phase. Blocked at the oral level, Renee had never experienced this pinnacle in libidinal evolution and it yet remained to be surmounted. This was accomplished easily and normally. Earlier, by persistence and by a vivacity of spirit she had tried to capture the attention of the analyst's husband. When she was secure that she too enjoyed the love of the "father," she attempted to imitate the mother-analyst's behavior toward him, but always on a transposed feeling-grade. Nonetheless the sense of Oedipus guilt was present, revealed in a dream where, in the presence of the "father," Renee saw herself the victor in a debate with the mother-analyst who thereupon turned away from her. This was a normal phenomenon and her only anxiety dream with Oedipus content. Soon her attention turned to her professors and to her fellow students. She anticipated marriage and motherhood serenely, waiting happily for her Prince Charming.

In all aspects of human activity Renee reached the adult normal level, climbing an ascending road toward the simultaneous conquest of her ego and of reality, possible only through the gradual desubjectivization and decentralization of the ego.

In turn this liberation of the deep-rooted imprisoning egocentrism could be effected only by the mechanisms of symbolic projection and imitation. If these were to play a constructive role in the ego's reformation, they did so in proportion as they were allowed to make up for the initial frustrations, the original sources of the psychotic breakdown.

A Dynamic Conception of the Process of Disintegration in Schizophrenia

Throughout this study, an effort has been made to demonstrate the similarities between certain aspects of schizophrenic and infantile thinking. Because the schizophrenic disintegration greatly simplifies psychic processes, it has been possible to study formative mechanisms in the ego, which, not surprisingly, resemble those functioning in the small child. To all intents and purposes, the processes of projection and imitation through which the ego finds itself and distinguishes itself from the non-ego are employed as well by the child as by the schizophrenic. The question then arises whether a closer relationship may not be established between Piaget's conclusions about the child and those of the psychoanalysts. To reduce the schizophrenic mentality to that of the child would of course be an obvious mistake; too many dissimilarities intervene. Yet, in the presence of an illness effecting profound regression to the earliest evolutionary phases, the phenomena presented might be examined in the light of Piaget's theories. From this examination the valuable conclusion might be drawn that what seems to be a disintegrative process can, under certain conditions, become a reconstructive one. Indeed, all schizophrenics avail themselves of the mechanisms of projection, participation, condensation and imitation to express the psychic life.

Rather than allow them to remain at the service of destructive drives and delirious formulations, however, these mechanisms can be drawn on and utilized in efforts to reconstruct the psychotic ego. If in the child these processes constitute a normal and natural aspect of its affective-intellectual evolution, in the psychotic they serve the primordial function of sheltering the patient from frustrating reality and permitting the satisfaction of a basic need. The facets of this function must be more extensively studied with the objective of incorporating it in a new psychotherapy founded on the symbolic realization of the patient's fundamental wants.

It is to be hoped that this brief examination of the disintegration and reconstruction of a schizophrenic ego may serve to indicate the importance of recognizing the formative ego mechanisms in the psychotherapy of a schizophrenic. For if one aspect of the psychosis is characterized by the eruption of unconscious drives into the conscious life, the disintegration of the ego seems to be one of the principal causes of this usurpation by the unconscious. For this reason, psychoanalysts and psychogeneticists, instead of working separately, should on the contrary attempt a synthesis of their respective methods, a synthesis which would prove directly beneficial to the clinician in his treatment of schizophrenics.

Bibliography

FREUD, SIGMUND: Nouvelles conférences sur la Psychanalyse. Paris, Gallimard, p. vi.

LAVELLE, LOUIS: De l'être. Quoted by Foulquié, P.: L'Existentialisme. Paris, Presses Universitaires de France, p. 128.

ODIER, CHARLES: L'angoisse et la pensée magique. Neuchâtel, Delachaux and Niestlé, 1948. P. 103.

PIAGET, JEAN: La formation du symbole chez l'enfant. Neuchâtel, Delachaux and Niestlé, 1948. P. 113.

———: La construction du réel chez l'enfant. Neuchâtel, Delachaux and Niestlé, 1948. P. 121.

PICHON, EDOUARD: La personne et la personnalité vues à la lumière de la pensée idiomatique française. Rev. franç. de psychanalyse 10: 117, 1938.

SECHEHAYE, MARGUERITE: La réalisation symbolique (nouvelle méthode de psychothérapie appliquée à un cas de schizophrénie). Rev. suisse d. psychol. et d. psychol. appliquée (Suppl.) 5: 17, 27, 87, 88, 102.

DE SAUSSURE, FERDINAND: Cours de linguistique générale. Edited by Bailly, Charles, and Sechehaye, Albert. Lausanne and Paris, Payot, 1916. P. 130.

INDEX

Activity
  in dispelling anxiety, 27
  in restoring reality, 38
Adualism, 144
Affective realism, 150
Aggression, 47, 145
  expressed in symbols, 114-115
  projection of, 145
Analyst
  fear of, 51
  incorporation into, 124-126
  loss of contact with, 100
  methods used by, 54
  reassurance offered by, 41, 52-53, 57, 58
  relations with, 48, 49-50, 59-60, 76-79, 87-89, 93-94, 104-123, 127-129, 147, 153, 156-162, 164-168, 169-171, 173-176
  and the "System," 89
Anemophilia, 31
Anemophobia, 32-33, 145
Anger, expressed symbolically, 115
Anxiety, 143
  created by school subjects, 28-30
  dispelled by activity, 27
  experience of, on street, 29
  at play, 23-25
  in principal's office, 25-26
  in relation to a teacher, 26
  in sanatarium, 30-34
  and the "System's" orders, 67
  on unreality, 83
  See also Fear
Apathy, 80, 116, 119
Apples, 98-99, 100-102, 103-108
Automatism, 91

Bathing, 109-110
Body, interest in, 109, 127
Body-ego, 179-182
  construction of, 169-180
Breasts, represented by apples, 104-108

Catatonia, 116-117, 118
  dispelling of, 123
Calisthenics, 28-29
Cathexis, 146-147

Death-instinct, 151
Delirium, 145
Departure, expressed symbolically, 115
Direction, sense of, 88, 172
Disassociation, 134
Dolls, reaction to, 39-42, 122-123
Drawing, reaction to, 29
Dream, 184

"the needle in the hay,"
23-24
Drives, 140

Eating, 76, 115
Echo-acousia, 25-26
Ego, 128
  body-awareness, 179-182
  body-awareness construc-
    tion, 169-171
  and capacity for imita-
    tion, 165-166
  disintegration of, 139-155
  eruption of the uncon-
    scious into, 146
  and hallucinations, 148
  and introjection of
    maternal love, 149
  and object relationships,
    142
  oral construction, 161-169
  and primary drives, 145
  and projection, 149-151
  reconstruction of, 156-176
  regression of, to fetal
    stage, 153-160
  and society, 142
  and weaning, 140

Fantasies, 58-59
Fear, 32-35, 135
  during analysis, 45
  madness as escape from,
    43
  of psychoanalyst, 51
  See also Anxiety
Fixation, at weaning period,
  140
Freud, 149

Guilt, 47-49, 93, 94, 99, 115-
121
  augmented by pain, 124
  aroused by pleasure, 110

Hallucinations, auditory,
26, 50, 59, 70, 81, 92,
95, 99-101, 115, 116, 120-
121, 125, 148-149
Hands, 99
Hate, 47
Hostility, to psychoanalyst,
112
  See also Aggression

Id, 148
"Imago," creation of, 161-
162
Imitation, 183
  in ego construction, 179
  in ego reconstruction, 164-
    168
  in infant, 163
Infant, projection, 163
Introjection, maternal,
166, 167-168

"Land of Enlightenment,"
49
  and madness, 62-63, 68
Language, self-created, 113,
120
Lavelle, L., 181
Libido, 181-182
  and destructive drives, 151
  in schizophrenia, 142

Madness
  and "enlightenment," 62-
    63, 67
  as escape from fear, 43
  and unreality, 44
Masochism, 150
Milk, 108
Mother, 143
  and reality, 144
Mother-feeding, 151, 152

"Needle in the hay," a
dream, 24
Noises, inner, 59
  See also Hallucinations

Non-ego, 144, 154

Objects
  cathexis, 146
  interrelationships of, and
    the ego, 147
Odier, C., 150
Oedipus phase, 182-183
Orality, 152-153

Pain, 134-135
  augmentation of guilt, 124
Personality, maintaining
  integrity of, 58, 65
Personification, 134
Perspective (spatial), 172
  and ego-synthesis, 142
  loss of, 29, 88
Piaget, J., 163
Projection, 182
  in creation of a new
    "Imago," 161-162
  in ego construction, 179
  as ego defense, 144-146,
    149-150
  in infant, 163
Psychoanalyst. See Analyst
Psychosis. See Schizo-
  phrenia
Punishment, 60, 96, 99,
  desire for, 48-49
  See also Self-destruction

Realism, affective, 150
Reality
  oral sources of, 152-153
  pathological perception of,
    139-144
  regaining of, 130-136
  structuration of, 171-176
  See also Unreality
Regression, 99, 154, 178

Schizophrenia
  disintegration of ego,
    139-155
  mechanism in, 185-187

regression to fetal stage,
  153-158
Self-awareness, and imita-
  tion, 162-163
Self-destruction, 90, 93, 96,
  100, 115-116, 121, 150-151
Self-preservation, 147
Sewing, reaction to, 29
Singing, reaction to, 28-29
Stupor, 116, 119
Suicide. See Self-destruction
Super-ego, 150
Symbols, 135-136
  of aggression, 115
"System" (the), 48-49, 51,
  77-78
  and the analyst, 89-90
  loss of interest in, 121
  orders issued by, 57-60, 65-
    67, 76, 89-90, 92, 95
  role of, 146-147

Temperature, 42
Tension of unreality, 115

Unconscious, eruption of,
  into ego, 146
Unreality
  anxiety of, 67
  feeling of, at schook, 25-26
  first feeling of, 21-22
  decrease of, 30-31, 105-
    106, 129
  and madness, 44
  representation of, 44
  struggle against, 35-36
  tension of, expressed
    symbolically, 115
  and "things," 55-57
  See also Reality

Voices, inner. See Hallucinations

Weaning, 140
Wind, reaction to, 32-33